"After reading *Sacred Intent*, I truly [...] equipped to use your influence for [...] lost, build healthy life-giving relation[...] principles of God's Word, and manage your time so you can dream big, God-sized visions and accomplish the calling God has for you."

Tom Mullins
Founding pastor of Christ Fellowship and president of EQUIP

"In *Sacred Intent* Brent Crowe has produced a model for viewing and approaching life that will allow any Christ follower to accomplish exponentially more than they ever thought possible!"

Brad Lomenick
Leadership consultant and speaker, former president of Catalyst,
and author of *The Catalyst Leader* and *H3 Leadership*

"You have one shot in your life. It is not a dress rehearsal. Your time is now. Maximizing your moments in life will set you apart from others, and *Sacred Intent* will show you how to do it. Get it. Read it. Tell your friends about it."

Dr. Ronnie Floyd | President of the Southern Baptist Convention
and senior pastor of Cross Church

"Brent Crowe has the unique ability to take complicated concepts and explain them in a way all of us can understand. In *Sacred Intent* he performs his 'magic' once again, providing us with a manual for faithful discipleship that is insightful, engaging, and practical."

Daniel L. Akin | President of Southeastern Baptist Theological Seminary

"Like Brent Crowe, I believe you are capable of so much more than you may believe. Do you want to make a difference in your generation? Do you want to learn how to live your life in a way that positively influences people for eternity? If so, *Sacred Intent* will be one of your most helpful tools along the way."

Sean McDowell, Ph.D.
Professor at Biola University, speaker, and best-selling author of
more than fifteen books, including *Is God Just a Human Invention?*

"Updates for apps and games improves your experience with them. That's exactly what Dr. Brent Crowe's book *Sacred Intent* will do for your life! We're prone to get stuck in the buffering ideas of the past, but Dr. Crowe offers a change of thought. Every chapter will help link you up to a future that looks awesome—really awesome!"

Tony Nolan | Gospel preacher

"In *Sacred Intent* Brent Crowe posits that being created in the *imago Dei* necessitates a responsibility to lead. The question is not whether one *should* lead, but whether one *will* lead. With biblical impetus, cogent logic, and a readable style, Crowe both challenges and encourages Christian leaders and their aspirants to fulfill God's sacred intent for them."

Rick Brewer, PhD | President of Louisiana College

"So much of church discipleship focuses on the lowest common denominator: offering truth that pretty much anyone can grasp. In *Sacred Intent*, Brent Crowe offers a great resource for those with a deeper thirst for God."

Alvin L. Reid
Southeastern Baptist Theological Seminary Professor of Evangelism
and Student Ministry/Bailey Smith Chair of Evangelism

"In *Sacred Intent* Brent Crowe affords readers the opportunity to shrink life into a manageable paradigm that will then allow them to maximize their moments in faithful obedience to God. Timely and a must-read, it equips readers to think with biblical discernment in an effort to tell a compelling story with the time and life they've been granted."

Pat Williams | Senior VP of the Orlando Magic

"*Sacred Intent* is a challenging, inspiring, and life-changing book based on biblical truths for those who wish to maximize their potential for Christ. I found myself reaching for new horizons and setting clear personal and professional goals."

Dr. Jairy Hunter | President of Charleston Southern University

"Brent Crowe has captured the essence of the biblical model of communicating truth. Chapter by chapter he masterfully moves from principle to practice. *Sacred Intent* defines for us what should be considered the normal Christian life."

Mike Calhoun | Executive assistant to the president of Word of Life

"In *Sacred Intent,* Brent Crowe has accomplished the much-needed but rare task of connecting the dots between rich theology and daily practice. This is for those with a deep well of motivations simply needing a mental map and model by which to channel their efforts."

Dr. Jack Graham | Pastor of Prestonwood Baptist Church

"In Brent Crowe's new book, *Sacred Intent,* you will be encouraged in your leadership potential. His truth and principles will lift your heart to embrace God's best in your calling as you faithfully run in the lane Christ has marked out for you."

Johnny Hunt | Author, speaker, and pastor of First Baptist Woodstock

"In a day where Christian celebrities dominate the spotlight, Brent Crowe shows us that God still delights in using ordinary people for extraordinary purposes. *Sacred Intent* is for anyone who feels common but longs to be used in uncommon ways."

Max Davis | Author of *Dead Dog Like Me*

"In *Sacred Intent,* Brent Crowe powerfully lays out a strategy and game plan to change your world. Read it, act on its principles, and shake the world for good. All of us have what it takes if we will trust in God's exceedingly abundant power."

Jonathan Falwell | Pastor of Thomas Road Baptist Church

"With great insight and personal reflection, Brent Crowe draws from biblical texts and characters to address one of today's greatest discipleship threats—a compartmentalized faith. In contrast, Brent champions for an *all-in* journey with Jesus through sacred stewardship of our lives."

David Ferguson, DPhil, DLitt | Great Commandment Network

SACRED INTENT

MAXIMIZE THE MOMENTS OF YOUR LIFE

BRENT CROWE, PH. D.

WORTHY®
PUBLISHING

Published by Worthy Books, an imprint of Worthy Publishing Group, a division of Worthy Media, Inc., One Franklin Park, 6100 Tower Circle, Suite 210, Franklin, TN 37067.

WORTHY is a registered trademark of Worthy Media, Inc.

HELPING PEOPLE EXPERIENCE THE HEART OF GOD

eBook available wherever digital books are sold.

Library of Congress Control Number: 2015945246

For foreign and subsidiary rights, contact rights@worthypublishing.com

Published in association with Ted Squires Agency, Nashville, Tennessee

ISBN: 978-1-61795-601-0

Cover Design: Micah Kandross

Printed in the United States of America
15 16 17 18 19 LBM 8 7 6 5 4 3 2 1

For all the students who have ever attended
Student Leadership University;
for all the pastors, youth workers, educators,
and parents who made a way for the journey;
and for the millions of lives they will impact.

CONTENTS

Prologue: Matthias and Justus Are My Homies   1

Monday: INFLUENCE   7
Introduction: A Great Day for a Sacred Do-Over   9
1. Influence and the World of the Lost Beginning   11
2. Between Two Prayers: Leadership in Transition   26
3. Between Two Worlds: Thoughts While Leaving Earth   41

Tuesday: TIME   57
Introduction: Costly Grace and a Faustian Bargain   59
4. Time Understood: Stories Within the Story   64
5. Time Purposed: Living Life's Last Cigarette   72
6. Time Managed: Redeeming the Time   77

Wednesday: CALLING   89
Introduction: Stay in Your Own Lane   91
7. Going Retro with the Reformers   93
8. A Hypocrite's Confession   108

Thursday: ENGAGEMENT   117
Introduction: Marinating Metaphors   119
9. Salt: The Fellowship of the Concerned   122
10. Light: The Fellowship of Illumination   129
11. The Wayback Machine   135

Friday: RELATIONSHIPS   143
Introduction: Rocket Ships and Candy   145
12. Doctors and Patients   150
13. Collaboration: We > Me   166

Saturday: MOTIVATIONS   177
Introduction: Invisible Labor   179
14. I Am a Giant Killer   181
15. I'm On an Adventure   195

Sunday: DREAMING   203
Introduction: A Perfect Day for the Impossible   205
16. The Day Mack the Turtle Boldly Burped   207
17. To Change the World   216

Conclusion: 7 Days, 7 Passports, 7 Questions   235

Appendix: Sacred Intent Reflections and Prayers   239
Notes   254

MATTHIAS AND JUSTUS ARE MY HOMIES

Very little is known concerning Matthias and Justus. Some of us may not even be able to recall where their names are mentioned in Scripture. After Jesus ascended to heaven, the eleven apostles, along with Jesus' family and some of the women who had faithfully served him, went back to Jerusalem and gathered in the Upper Room. The purpose of this gathering was to replace Judas Iscariot, who had put a monetary value on his faithfulness to Jesus. He had betrayed our Lord for thirty pieces of silver and, overcome with grief and remorse, committed suicide by hanging himself. Peter and the other ten apostles believed that the Scriptures required that the twelfth office of apostle, formerly held by Judas, be filled. Narrowing down the field was easy. There were two men who had been present throughout the entire ministry of Jesus from his baptism on. Their names were Joseph called Barsabbas, who was also called Justus, and Matthias (Acts 1:23). Choosing between the two men would be the more difficult task, making what comes next a bit strange:

> And they prayed and said, "You, Lord, who know the
> hearts of all, show which one of these two you have chosen

to take the place in this ministry and apostleship from which Judas turned aside to go to his own place." And they cast lots for them, and the lot fell on Matthias, and he was numbered with the eleven apostles. (Acts 1:24–26)

Now, the praying part makes complete sense to me, but to roll dice feels a bit Star-Wars-mind-trick-esque. While this may seem like the disciples were leaving the most important office, that of apostle, to the movement of chance, in reality this was an ancient custom. In truth, God would be the one to determine the outcome. An ancient way of doing this would be to mark stones, some with Matthias's name and some with Justus's, and place them in a jar. The jar would then be shaken, and the name on the stone that fell out first was the one chosen as the twelfth apostle.[1]

I think a lot of Christians have a hard time relating to Noah and a flood that destroyed the entire world, Moses leading two million people across the Red Sea, or Daniel standing for his faith and spending the night in a pit of lions. Most of us also have a hard time relating to rock star Christians who are famous athletes, have their own reality television shows, or give a testimony of being a big-time drug addict until a Damascus-road-type experience. Most of us will never lead two million people or have our own show on cable, and we've never seen a flashing supernatural light. Most of us came to Jesus not because he has a booming, loud, James Earl Jones–type voice, but because he whispered through the chaos of our existence, "Come and follow me."

Many have a difficult time with "Christian fame" as the ideal to strive for, and we are just trying to graduate and get into a good university or maybe earn enough money to send our kids to college or are looking for a job that will fulfill us. We love Jesus and want to follow him with the entirety of our lives. So we understand the obscurity of Matthias and Justus. They were faithful and followed Jesus, but their names never appeared in lights like Peter's or John's.

This book is for all the Matthiases and Justuses of the world, not the Johns and Peters . . . they're busy writing their own books. This is for normal people who live seemingly normal lives and want to make those lives count. For those who get picked last but possess first-round-pick potential. Those of us who only get a shot because the dice were rolled and we were tapped on the shoulder by supernatural chance. Yeah, that's me, and Matthias and Justus are my homies. There is something very liberating about not being chosen in the first, second, or hundredth round but still having the doors of opportunity swing open to us. This is for those who always play on the sandlot but are still pointing to the stands like Babe Ruth on a clear day, for those who look into the face of disparaging odds and simply wink.

So if you are a normal person and want to live a life well for the audience of God, then the following pages were written with you in mind. But before we proceed, let me offer a brief word of caution. I cannot motivate you. If you lack motivation, then this book is not for you. You need another book, maybe read the Bible . . . and if that does not work, read it again. I am writing for those, no matter their age, who want to fan the flame of motivation. Who want to matter and need a plan for their "want to."

I will never forget sitting in the Royal Automobile Club in London, England, almost ten years ago. The walls were ornate with distinguished paintings honoring the upper class of society. Every sound bounced off the stonewalls and granite flooring that you would expect to find in such a dignified establishment. There were rooms dedicated to playing cards, others to reading newspapers or smoking pipes and cigars. And on this particular day, about three hundred young leaders from the States involved with Student Leadership University (SLU) and I found ourselves in an upstairs ballroom awaiting presentations from our host, Prince Michael of Kent; Sir Nicholas Soames, who is a member of Parliament; and a third gentleman named Dr. Graham Lacey. Dr. Lacey is a longtime family friend and one of the most entertaining storytellers I have ever been privileged to listen to.

We were having a great afternoon, and the students were thriving in this environment and interacting with leaders from another country. They asked great questions from Prince Michael and thoroughly enjoyed hearing stories from Mr. Soames concerning his grandfather, who happens to have been Winston Churchill. But it was the final presentation of the day that left an enduring impression on my mind. Dr. Lacey took to the platform and began with a simple statement followed by a profound question: "Students, I want you to imagine that the whole of your life is a week. Shrink your life into seven days, and now consider the day you are presently living. If life is a week, then you as a seventeen- or eighteen-year-old young person are probably finishing up Tuesday and looking to begin Wednesday." He confessed that his stage of life was much more advanced, saying, "I wrestle with the notion that I am most likely on Friday and closing in on Saturday." He then discussed the brevity of life and concluded with these words: "Life is a week. How will you make all seven days count?"

And so it is that the following pages are written with a very similar paradigm in mind. If life were a week, then we understand our energy to be limited, thus we must be good stewards of our human experience. My desire is to offer you a mental map and model for focusing the *want to* in your life so that you can live a life of sacred intent. My hope is that this paradigm will shrink life into something manageable that can be accomplished and completed. I am not suggesting that a life of sacred intent doesn't need God. But rather, to live with a sacred intent simply means that we seek to be exhaustively intentional, understanding that God gifts each moment to us. Therefore, each day of the week will serve as a different emphasis:

- Monday: *Influence*
- Tuesday: *Time*
- Wednesday: *Calling*
- Thursday: *Engagement*
- Friday: *Relationships*
- Saturday: *Motivation*
- Sunday: *Dream*

Seven is the number of completeness, and a life rich with sacred intent will be complete. So let us begin, because the clock is ticking and the calendar pages are turning . . . and your moment is now!

MONDAY

INFLUENCE

INTRODUCTION

A GREAT DAY FOR A SACRED DO-OVER

CHAPTER ONE

**INFLUENCE AND THE WORLD OF
THE LOST BEGINNING**

CHAPTER TWO

**BETWEEN TWO PRAYERS:
LEADERSHIP IN TRANSITION**

CHAPTER THREE

**BETWEEN TWO WORLDS:
THOUGHTS WHILE LEAVING EARTH**

A GREAT DAY FOR A SACRED DO-OVER

Monday is a great day for beginnings. For me it is a day that I commit to exercise and/or eat right a certain amount that week. It's like my own mini New Year's Day in which I can make resolutions and hope for the best. Maybe I like Mondays because the do-over I get reminds me of the grace I do not deserve. In any case, no matter the calendar day or the chronology of your years, I want you to read the next three chapters with a do-over mind-set. Give yourself permission to start anew. If you don't, the following information will be just . . . information. However, if you permit yourself to start again, what you read will go beyond informative and will become transformative. So it's a good day to start something or, for our purposes, to start believing something about ourselves.

We begin our discussion of sacred intentions with the first day of the week and the first book of the Bible, where an influence was granted humans in the world of the lost beginning. *Genesis*, after all, means "beginning" or "in the beginning" in both Greek and Hebrew, and the main theme of the book has to do with origins. While the focus of Genesis is the origin of the created world, the human race, the numerous nations of the earth, and the covenant family through which the redeemer would be born,[1] it is also the origin of something else: influence. In Genesis, all of God's creation is pregnant with potential and possibility. My hope is that as you read the following chapters that comprise Monday, you will awaken to the leadership potential that exists in you. I write with a sanctified optimism that once we awaken to how we were created and gifted, we will begin to see our own lives afresh and pregnant with possibility to accomplish the desires of God.

God has designed people to have influence and to lead. Once we establish this idea, our attention will then turn to two great biblical examples of leadership at work. First, we will dedicate careful attention to the Old Testament relationship between Moses and young Joshua; and second, we will evaluate the New Testament paradigm of how Paul developed Timothy.

Pretty much any book on leadership will affirm the belief that to lead is to influence. And in many cases, those with the greatest amount of influence are willing to sacrifice the most for their cause. So we will begin with the origin of influence in the Creation story. Why? Because Genesis is the beginning that is the beginning of every story, and in order to fully grasp the purpose of our influence, we must see ourselves in the origin of it all. Then we will become convinced that, though disfigured by sin, the residue of God's purpose still exists, is still discernable, and is still applicable.

So here we are . . . it's Monday, no matter when you are reading this, and last week is ancient history. You are on the precipice of your future, and the vantage point allows you to see and shape your own future. You can capture these moments with a sacred sense of intentionality. So get ready, because we are jumping into the deep end of the pool, and we left the floaties in the closet at home.

CHAPTER ONE

INFLUENCE AND THE WORLD OF THE LOST BEGINNING

There is an age-old question that has been kicked around the block for as long as people have been writing on the subject of leadership: Are leaders born or are leaders made? And so we wrestle with such a question on Monday. Most answers have been largely based on one's context and culture, or rather some philosophy of leadership espoused and believed. I guess it would very much depend on when and where you were born as to your take on this seemingly overcomplicated and somewhat ambiguous query. For example, at certain times in history, one's bloodline would determine one's place in society; at other times, being female or a certain ethnicity would automatically disqualify one from leadership.

But therein lies the rub and evolving tension concerning the matter of who can actually be a leader. Because most reading these words would take serious offense to the notion that one is disqualified from leading due to bloodlines, sex, or ethnicity. We have the benefit of living in a time and place when influence has not been segregated for a select few. We have been born in a Western context, which means there are some safe assumptions that can be made.

First, Westerners seem to be born equipped with a rugged

individualism and initiative that has sometimes been described as "ready, shoot, aim." Second, the Western mind-set is one that can think for itself rather than simply accepting traditions or beliefs. Additionally, embedded into the Western DNA is a desire to work toward and serve a greater good, and in doing so accomplish something that can be measured. In other words, there is a bit of an entrepreneurial spirit in all of us (sometimes for better and sometimes for worse).

I simply point this out because the Western mind-set is much more apt to believe the following statements: "I am a leader" or "I can become a leader." Our way of thinking is positively susceptible to the notion of influence. In fact, I believe that our independent mind-set coupled with our initiative and desire to accomplish something measurable conditions us toward the whole idea. We are wired to think we matter and can make a difference.

LEADERSHIP POTENTIAL EXISTS IN EVERYONE

Most of my high school days began with me looking into the mirror in the morning and feeling defeated. The sixteen-year-old face staring back at me did not represent anything to get very excited about. I felt alone, ugly, weak, talentless, and all-around unappealing. No matter how you look at it, I was lost. I drifted the halls of my school largely unnoticed and never made a big impact on any sports team. My grades were below average, and my motivation toward life in general seemed almost nonexistent. Those close to me were typically clueless to my plight and to the dark cloud that seemed to hang over my head many days.

Twenty years later, my life is a very different scene. I have two master's degrees and a PhD; I am published, run a healthy organization, and have a busy speaking schedule. And infinitely more important, I have been married to Christina for thirteen years, and we have three amazing kids. While I could blush on and on, filling books in an effort to describe how happy and grateful I am for my family, the point is that something fundamental about my thinking has changed somewhere in the last two decades. You see, around my senior year, I started to love Jesus. And I mean I really started to love Jesus, not in a "show up every Sunday" kind of way, but as if my life were a living, breathing, walking, mega worship song sung on a daily basis kind of way.

It is quite amazing the difference a personal relationship with Jesus makes in someone's life. Out of all the things that were transformed in me, the most fundamental was the motivation, the why, of my life. Jesus in my life brought with him a sacred intent, a motivation that altered the trajectory of my story. And so it was that I began to think differently, or better yet, something else was now beginning to serve as a filter for my thoughts. That something was truth. Truth, or it could also be called theology, began to inform how I viewed myself. The presence of Jesus afforded me the ability to experience truth and have a healthy theology, which in turn informed my practice. The sixteen-year-old version of me viewed the person in the mirror through the chaotic white noise and emotions of being broken and in a state of fallenness. Today I view myself through the grid of what God says and thinks about me. Truth and theology are essential to defining and determining my perspective.

That is why I believe there are reasons beyond culture and context—when and where you were born—that explain why leadership potential exists in every human. The grand narrative of

Scripture, expressing God's desires for humanity, far outweighs any other factors in determining why we are created to influence. God's story is the great beacon of light shining meaning and clarity on each and every story told through the human condition and experience. Therefore, I want to offer four reasons why we as followers of Jesus should believe we possess a measure of leadership potential and capacity.

Reason #1: You Were Created in the Image of God

Attempting to understand what it means to be made in the image of God is a monumental task. To do so we must return to what Dietrich Bonhoeffer referred to as "the world of the lost beginning" where mankind was created and made sense. Our purpose is to simply understand the consequence of being made in the image of God as it relates to our influence in God's creation.

> Then God said, "Let us make man in our image, after our likeness. And let them have dominion over the fish of the sea and over the birds of the heavens and over the livestock and over all the earth and over every creeping thing that creeps on the earth." So God created man in his own image, in the image of God he created him; male and female he created them. (Genesis 1:26–27)

We are the pinnacle of God's creation. While this may sound a bit egotistical or self-centered, I assure you that it is simply an inescapable conclusion. Since we are made in the image of God and thus designated as the crown of God's creation, we can conclude that *human beings were created to influence*.

The Latin phrase *imago Dei* is translated "the image of God." And while there is some measure of mystery surrounding the meaning of God's image and likeness in man, it is safe to conclude human beings are godlike to some degree. Now, this doesn't indicate we are as smart as God, for the devil and the angels have a superior intellect to mankind and they are not created in the image of God. Nor does it mean we physically look like God, for God is spirit. And certainly we are not immortal and eternal in the same sense that God is immortal and eternal, for we have a beginning and in some sense an end, though we live on in a glorified state for eternity.[2]

To be made in the image of God seems to refer to the fact that God has created us to be like him and to represent him in creation. Adam and Eve, who were the only part of creation made with the capacity and privilege to walk and talk with God in the garden of Eden, were given specific responsibilities (Genesis 2:15, 19). The writer of Ecclesiastes offers further clarification: "God made men and women true and upright; *we're* the ones who've made a mess of things" (7:29 MSG).

In the same statement that God spoke of making man in his image and likeness, he also spoke of him having "dominion" over all of creation. Essentially, God has given mankind an active, authoritative role within his creation to fulfill his desires and will. The psalmist articulated this truth beautifully:

Yet we've so narrowly missed being gods,
    bright with Eden's dawn light.
You put us in charge of your handcrafted world,
    repeated to us your Genesis-charge,

Made us lords of sheep and cattle,
    even animals out in the wild,
Birds flying and fish swimming,
    whales singing in the ocean deeps.
GOD, brilliant Lord,
    your name echoes around the world.
(Psalm 8:5–9 MSG)

We are stewards of God's creation, and his name should echo through our influence around the world. Isn't that incredible? We no longer need to ask, "Are leaders born or made?" and "Can I be a leader?" Instead, our questions should be, "How can God's desired will be fulfilled through my influence?" and "How does my influence reverberate God's name for all to hear and experience?"

Reason #2: God Gave Us Freedom, Relationship, and Creativity

I love Christmas morning with all its traditions, surprises, and chaos. I love the smells, the tree that is still hanging on since we purchased it the day after Thanksgiving, the silly Christmas-themed jammies, and kids shredding paper in sheer delight. While all of the aforementioned things are fun and great, central in all these traditions is the celebration of the birth of Jesus. In our house, on any given year, there are three to four nativity sets my wife places throughout the home. There is one that is actually a painting of little children reenacting the nativity scene wearing old bed sheets and using house pets as props. Then there is one made of olive wood that I purchased from Bethlehem years ago; another, a plastic figure set that the kids and I can play with; and a ceramic figurine set that neither the kids nor I are allowed to touch. And all these nativities exist to remind our family that the greatest gift ever given was Emmanuel, "God with us."

But long before the star appeared in the sky and the Magi from afar brought three gifts to baby King Jesus, there were three other gifts given to humanity. These cannot be called "Christmas gifts" because Jesus had not yet moved into the neighborhood of humanity. They can more accurately be referred to as "creation gifts" and, just like Jesus, they are available to all of humanity. Since God created us with the capacity and responsibility to influence, we need to take a closer look at these three particular gifts he gave to all mankind. When properly examined, these gifts help us better understand the influence God expects from his sons and daughters. Maybe in some small way I hope the creation gifts stir within you the same sense of wonder and excitement that a little kid feels walking down the hallway to the den on a Christmas morning.

Freedom. We live in a culture of misunderstood freedom. Freedom seems to have become something we feel *entitled to* rather than *endowed with.* It is an idea devoid of consequence and responsibility, defined completely by one's creative thought and inclination. If we feel it about ourselves, then we can believe it about ourselves. If we believe it about ourselves, then we authorize ourselves. And if we authorize ourselves, then *we* view ourselves as *the authority.* For obvious reasons this is a dangerous road paved with prideful intentions, and one on which Adam and Eve walked right out of Eden and into their permanent sabbatical.

So how should we define the gift of freedom as it is seen in the creation narrative? Genesis 2:16–17 (NKJV) articulates three distinguishing components:

1. A *respect* for the authority of God's words: "And the LORD God commanded man, saying . . ."
2. A *responsibility* to stay within the boundaries outlined by the words of God: "Of every tree of the garden you may freely eat; but of the tree of the knowledge of good and evil you shall not eat . . ."
3. *Consequences* for crossing the stated boundaries: "for in the day that you eat of it you shall surely die."[3]

In many ways the story of creation is a tale of freedom granted, manipulated, and destroyed. In my book *Chasing Elephants: Wrestling with the Gray Areas of Life*, I demonstrate how it is essential to understand one's freedom in order to make moral and God-honoring decisions. Our influence is thoroughly affected by our decision making, thus the ability to make decisions rightly is part of a bridge to healthy leadership.

Relationship. It's fascinating that the first problem in creation is not sinfulness but rather loneliness. God had repeatedly declared that his creation was good, but even before man's rebellion in chapter 3, we see in chapter 2 that it was "not good" for Adam to be alone. Had God made a mistake? Surely not, but God here shows that creation was incomplete prior to his gift of relationship. And not just any relationship. God created a companion . . . a wife; as most translations read, a "helper."

It is obvious that God created us to be social beings. It may sound a bit strange, but if God created me to be social, then I cannot be fully human by being alone. God did not create Adam with a relational need and then say, "Man, that guy is weak! Let's make him stronger by creating a wife." No, God created us relational because *he* is relational and we are made in his image.

God's original design was also for two people to become one flesh and create one family (1 male + 1 female = 1 family). And here we connect the dots with our discussion on leadership because families are the original creators of culture. Edgar H. Schein in his book *Organizational Culture and Leadership* wrote, "Culture is both a 'here and now' dynamic phenomenon and a coercive background structure that influences us in multiple ways . . . When we are influential in shaping the behavior and values of others, we think of that as 'leadership.'"[4] God created humans so that our values and behaviors would be shaped within the context of relationship. And relationships are the "here and now" through which culture is shaped.

Creativity. Until recently, creativity, or imagination, has been the most overlooked part of the creation narrative in my life. I never saw myself as very creative or artistic. My hobbies have never included painting or singing or sculpting, and the list could go on. I have always been more of the go-outside-and-throw-a-ball or catch-a-fish kind of guy. Tucked away in these two short verses, though, is a statement that demonstrates humans are creative— even me!

So the LORD God formed from the ground all the wild animals and all the birds of the sky. He brought them to the man to see what he would call them, and the man chose a name for each one. He gave names to all the livestock, all the birds of the sky, and all the wild animals. (Genesis 2:19–20 NLT)

God created all the animals and then brought them to Adam "to see what he would call them."

God wasn't wondering what Adam would name them because he didn't know, for that would fall under a theological belief called *open theism*, which holds the idea that the future is not yet known to God and is subject to change. This presents an obvious challenge to the historical understanding of God being omniscient, or all knowing. The late Dr. Bill Bright, in his book *God: Discover His Character*, wrote, "Because God knows absolutely everything that can ever be known . . . He is never bewildered or confused or perplexed . . . Nothing ever turns out differently than He expected or planned."[5]

The prophet Isaiah is particularly helpful in understanding that God is all knowing when he wrote, "I am God, and there is none like me, declaring the end from the beginning and from ancient times things not yet done, saying, 'My counsel shall stand, and I will accomplish all my purpose'" (Isaiah 46:9–10).

If God looks down upon time, seeing the beginning, middle, and end, then we must conclude that he had always known what name Adam would give to each animal. He just wanted Adam to use his creativity to accomplish the task. Adam was required to use his imagination to rule over the animals, and God delighted in his obedience. Therefore, imagination as a gift can be understood as the use of creative energy, within the context of God's creation, to fulfill God's purposes.

How will you use your freedom to navigate and make decisions in this world? What types of marriages, friendships, and communities can be formed from a healthy view of relationship? And what kind of imaginative possibilities are waiting to be discovered because of your creativity? God certainly gifted the crown of his creation with all that was necessary to influence well.

Reason #3: Leadership As Part of Discipleship

Over the previous twenty-plus years, shelves have been annually stocked afresh with the latest books and resources to help people tap into their leadership ability. And while there are seemingly as many leadership titles as there are stars in the sky, Christ followers need to be cautious.

When someone in a Christian context tosses around the word *leader*, it doesn't mean the same thing as *disciple*. Those terms are not synonymous and should never be used interchangeably, so we must wrestle with their true meanings because a wrong word can communicate the wrong message. Furthermore, communicating the wrong message can lead to unhealthy conclusions that may smother potential influence.

For example, there are certain cultures in the world where I do not refer to myself as a Christian because it could conjure up a stereotypical image of people in the West who have waged wars on certain Arab people throughout history. I therefore refer to myself as a follower of Jesus, taking the time to explain what that means. Only after a relationship is established do I try to redeem the term *Christian* in their minds.

The word *disciple* is taken from the Greek *mathētēs* and is used to refer, in a broad sense, to followers of a teacher such as Jesus or Paul (Matthew 10:24; Luke 14:26–27; John 4:1; 6:66). The term was also used to refer to the twelve apostles who followed Jesus. As disciples of Jesus Christ, we find in him the answer for the nothingness inside us, and once rescued, we love, obey, worship, and proclaim. We will even die for him. To reduce the whole of a disciple's newfound existence into trite or glossary-like statements would be like reducing falling in love and getting married to managing one's time well.

The disciple would rather have one minute experiencing God's grace than a lifetime of anything else. As Oswald Chambers has already written:

> Discipleship is based on devotion to Jesus Christ, rather than to an adherence to a belief or creed. "If any man comes to Me and does not hate . . . , he cannot be My disciple." There is no argument and no compulsion, but simply—If you would be my disciple, you must be devoted to Me. [6]

How, then, should disciples of Jesus view leadership? Certainly Scripture's emphasis on leadership and developing leaders cannot be ignored. Consider the airtime given to Moses and Joshua's relationship, Jesus and the Twelve, and Paul and Timothy. Paul even told Timothy that aspiring to positions of leadership in the church was a noble task (1 Timothy 3:1).

Thus, leadership is not something to be looked down upon by Christians, but rather it is to be sought and even desired, while at the same time filtered through the Scriptures. J. Oswald Sanders wrote, "Leadership is influence, the ability of one person to influence others to follow his or her lead."[7] Leadership development is the cultivating of one's influence as a disciple of Jesus for the glory of God.

There is a lot that goes into making a disciple and being a disciple, so it is very difficult to summarize and still capture its depth and width. In some measure, to summarize growing in my relationship with Jesus feels like I am cheapening the whole thing. How does one stop with one sentence when describing the type of devotion Chambers articulated? And that's the point. Describing devotion includes the full landscape of the relationship with all its obscurities, meaning, and beauty. The greatest description of the most beautiful thing still leaves one longing for more. And why? Because there is so much more to describe and so much more that words cannot describe. When we begin to feel the full weight of a disciple's devotion and depth of a sinner-saved-by-grace's gratitude, then even words become weak tools in an effort to describe.

As the disciples of old would sit at the feet of a teacher, so disciples of today should seek to live their lives at the feet of Jesus. If this is where the disciple spends his or her time, then this is where our leadership finds its meaning and motivation. Leadership begins at the feet of Jesus. The greatest reason, in the history of the universe, to lead and influence can only be discovered when we assume the posture of a time-gone-by disciple clamoring for a front-row mat on which to sit criss-cross applesauce to hear the voice of Jesus.

Here is one final thought in an effort to land the plane on the "disciple" and "leader" discussion. Every disciple should develop and exhaust his or her gifts to the fullest potential in an effort to have maximum influence for the glory of God. Thus, every disciple should lead with the understanding that influencing is part of the Christian journey. My hope here is that we continue to see *disciple* as a big, all-encompassing word that speaks to the entirety of the Christian journey in following Jesus. At the same time, my desire is that we begin to see *leader* as part of that journey. *Leadership* is part of, not separate from nor synonymous with, *discipleship*.

Reason #4: We're Part of the Mission of God

One of the more amazing aspects of the Christian journey is that we are allowed to take part in God's divine objective. Think about it: God is all about his mission, as he has demonstrated throughout human history. In fact, God is the first and ultimate missionary with his two greatest missionary acts. Missionary act #1 is the Bible:

> There's nothing like the written Word of God for showing you the way to salvation through faith in Christ Jesus. Every part of Scripture is God-breathed and useful one way or another—showing us truth, exposing our rebellion, correcting our mistakes, training us to live God's way. Through the Word we are put together and shaped up for the tasks God has for us. (2 Timothy 3:15–17 MSG)

And missionary act #2 is Jesus:

> The Word became flesh and blood,
> and moved into the neighborhood.

We saw the glory with our own eyes,
   the one-of-a-kind glory,
   like Father, like Son,
Generous inside and out,
   true from start to finish. (John 1:14 MSG)

If God is all about his mission, then the sacred intent of our lives should flow from this mission. Christopher Wright, author of *The Mission of God*, said that "the God who walks the paths of history through the pages of the Bible pins a mission statement to every signpost on the way," and the aim of every Christ follower should be "our committed participation as God's people, at God's invitation and command, in God's own mission within the history of God's world for the redemption of God's creation."[8]

When we take this mega-idea and couple it with other believers who also have been positioned to uniquely participate in God's mission, all our collective talents and abilities can be used to facilitate and further our involvement and influence in the mission of God. Whether you are athletically, artistically, or academically gifted, use your ability to make Jesus famous. This is the beauty of God's mission: God has tasked all of us to be collaborators, or coconspirators, for his purposes in his creation. You can have significant influence because the kingdom of God will have a worldwide impact. You can have a lasting effect because God will not and cannot fail in his mission. You can be a leader because God is a missionary.

CHAPTER TWO

BETWEEN TWO PRAYERS: LEADERSHIP IN TRANSITION

f ever a generation needed a guide, it is ours! Trying to study this generation is like walking into a room with millions of separate conversations taking place simultaneously. The only normal is change because every five minutes there is a technological breakthrough that will soon be a part of our daily rhythm. We seek to be spiritual, but not religious . . . retro, but not traditional . . . and full of conviction and cause, while we coexist and accommodate. We learn through images and media, making entertainment a primary means of education. And the ultimate goal, what we strive to attain the most, is an experience captured. To accomplish this we have all become photojournalists, sometimes even strapping a camera on a helmet or stick to record ourselves doing things. Yes, we are a generation where evolution is the norm, entertainment is the means, and experience is the goal. We are floating in a sea of digital white noise and need a guide. Someone who will help focus all the possibilities in our life toward a God-honoring end. The role of which I speak is that of mentor.

And so the purpose of this chapter is to survey the landscape of the relationship between Moses and Joshua to see what can be gleaned concerning a relational approach to leadership development. In examining the relational model of leadership development as it existed between Moses and young Joshua, we see Moses as the mentor and Joshua as the leader in training. Their relationship is one of the most important ones demonstrated for us in the Old Testament because Moses was preparing young Joshua to one day lead the nation of Israel. Throughout this chapter we will grapple with different aspects of the relationship between Moses and Joshua first, and then connect the dots from this ancient relationship to modern-day leadership development.

The life of Joshua was one born for the moment at hand. Just as Winston Churchill was born to defeat Hitler and will forever be known by his statement "Never give in!" so Joshua was born to lead the children of Israel into the promised land and will forever be known for fulfilling the orders from God to "be strong and courageous" (Joshua 1:9).

Joshua first appears on the scene in Exodus 17, but prior to this not much is known of his life or his family except that he was a prince in the tribe of Ephraim (Numbers 13:8, 16; Deuteronomy 32:44).[9] The name *Joshua* means "Jehovah is our help" and was given to him at the time he entered into Moses' service.

All the events of Moses and Joshua's relationship were bookended with prayer. Years before Deuteronomy 34, Moses had climbed up a hill and lifted his hands to pray over Joshua as he fought with the Amalekites; before he died, Moses laid hands upon him, officially transferring the leadership authority necessary to take Israel to the next stage in her journey. *Between those two prayers*, Joshua had experienced and been taught what it means to lead. In an effort to glean all that we can from Joshua and Moses' relationship, let's look at the four phases of one leader preparing another for leadership.

PHASE #1: LISTENING . . . AND FIGHTING IN THE VALLEY

The first event occurred in Exodus 17:8–16, just after the Amalekites had attacked Israel, when Moses said to Joshua, "Choose us some men and go out, fight with Amalek. Tomorrow I will stand on the top of the hill with the rod of God in my hand" (v. 9). This is the first mention of Joshua in Scripture, but we clearly see him portrayed as a military leader. It is quite possible that Joshua had served as Moses' assistant for a short time prior to this, but now the leader of Israel called upon the leader in training to carry out the significant task of defending his people. Up to this point, God had fought *for* Israel, but now God fought *through* Israel against the Amalekites, a formidable foe.

> The Amalekites, who appear here as the enemy of the Israelites, were a tough and aggressive Bedouin people who roamed the desert region of Sinai. Their nomadic existence led them to despise the settled and half-settled peoples who dwelt on the fringes of the desert, as the Israelites did. They thus robbed and harassed them, making themselves a serious threat to caravans and communities moving through the desert. In the age of David and Saul the Israelites living in the south of Judah were still troubled by the marauding raids of these Amalekites (1 Samuel 15; 27:8; 30:1ff) so that the Israelites and the Amalekites were in a permanent state of war.[10]

The following morning after the initial attack, Joshua did as Moses had commanded him and fought the Amalekites. During the battle, Moses, Aaron, and Hur went to the top of a hill overlooking the battlefield. There, Moses took his position holding the staff of God, with both hands raised toward heaven.[11] By stretching out his hands, Moses was demonstrating his dependence upon God for military victory. The Scriptures then say, "Whenever Moses held up his hand, Israel prevailed, and whenever he lowered his hand, Amalek prevailed" (Exodus 17:11).

Following the battle, the Scriptures note two things that Moses did. First, he recorded the event in a book so that it could be recounted later to Joshua that God would utterly and completely destroy Amalek. The intent was obvious. It was so Joshua "would be reminded of it, lest he should faint under the many difficulties which awaited him,"[12] as John Calvin wrote. Second, Moses built an altar, which he called "Jehovah my banner" or "The Lord is my Banner" to praise God for his help.[13] He did this so that all Israel could "testify, by solemn sacrifice, their gratitude; which the very name of the altar proves. For neither did he wish to erect a statue to God, nor to honour the altar by God's name, but he shows that this was the object he proposed to himself, that the Israelites being inflated by their good success, should not boast of their own strength, but the glory of God."[14]

The young man took away two great benefits from this incredible event. First, the opportunity and experience of leading the men into battle developed Joshua as a leader. While fulfilling such a task may sound overly simplistic, imagine the significant consequences had he failed at his first mention in history. Phase one of his leadership development took place in the national spotlight where success and failure would have been magnified due to public perception. The difference between how Joshua began his leadership journey and how many emerging leaders today are trained is light years apart. Joshua's mentor trained him with battle. Today he would have been assigned books to read and conferences to attend. I can only imagine that the lessons learned from spilling another man's blood left a far more indelible mark on Joshua than anything he could glean from a book or a motivational speaker.

Second, Joshua was taught that God granted the victory and it was not the result of human strength and strategy. This was the purpose behind recording the triumph in a book and building an altar, which would serve as continual reminders of God's sufficiency and promise. I believe the memory of this victory kept Joshua focused throughout his development and future leadership responsibilities.

What can we glean from Joshua listening and fighting in the valley that serves us well today in our leadership development? I believe there are three conclusions:

- Victory comes from above.
- Obedience to God will yield a richer experience of God's faithfulness.
- Documentation and memorials are important tools for remembering God's faithfulness and sufficiency.

It is quite fascinating when you think about the lessons from the valley. It is also quite liberating when you consider the burden of responsibility ultimately rests on God's shoulders. God granted success while Moses petitioned God and Joshua fought in the valley. I wonder how many of us would enjoy life more, that is to say have a richer and fuller experience, if we learned to pray, obey, and celebrate while completely trusting God to bless us with victory and success? God is on the mountain with the one praying and in the valley with the fighter. His presence is with the mentor and the emerging leader. In the end God wins; if you don't believe me, read Revelation 21:1–8! Along the way, God gives us little hints, like victory over the Amalekites, which are previews of the coming attraction that is his restoration of his creation.

PHASE #2: FOLLOWING UP THE MOUNTAIN

In Exodus 24:13 and then again in Exodus 32:15–17, Joshua accompanied Moses up and down Mount Sinai, the mountain of God, as Moses the intercessor met with God. This was a very important day in the history of the nation, so naturally Moses opted to take along his "intern." He could have taken Aaron or Hur or any of the elders, but he used this as another opportunity to develop his successor. Though it is not believed that Joshua ascended all the way up the mountain, he likely went at least a great distance with Moses and waited for him to come back down.[15]

During Moses' absence, Aaron and Hur were temporarily delegated the responsibility of overseeing the nation. No other individual is mentioned to have accompanied Moses up Sinai but Joshua. This was significant since Joshua's official position with Moses was as an assistant: "So Moses arose with his *assistant* Joshua, and Moses went up into the mountain of God" (Exodus 24:13, emphasis added). The word used here for "assistant" has two meanings. The first has to do with personal service rendered to an important person, usually a ruler; and the second refers to someone who served in the ministry of worship on the part of those who stand in a special relationship to God, such as the priests.[16] Joshua's services fell into both categories.

The event at Mount Sinai can serve as a microcosm of the mentor and emerging leader's relationship. Joshua's position, and the responsibilities that accompanied the role of assistant or servant, meant that he spent a large percentage of his time in Moses' presence. The routines of Moses' daily living and leading served as a platform for Joshua to be developed as a leader as they experienced life together.

Could you imagine being in such a close relationship with Moses? It is amazing to think of the backstage pass afforded to young Joshua. But that is the beauty of entering into a mentor-type relationship; the person being developed is given access that is off limits to others. I believe two conclusions can be made as it pertains to modern-day leadership development:

- A relationship is the best classroom for leadership development.
- Serving the leader, or shadowing a mentor, can be a catalyst for future leadership opportunities.

I have spent the last ten-plus years developing students to be leaders who see and act when all those around them operate with eyes wide shut. One of the challenges I continually place before them is to seek out a mentor, a leader who will invest in them on a personal level for the purpose of development. To enter into that type of relationship is, in essence, to walk into the best classroom available to learn how to influence. So let me challenge you to look around and make a list of people you would like to mentor you. Now, when some of us go to make this list, we immediately think, *Oh well, she is far too busy to have any time for someone like me.* Or, *Why would a guy running his own company give me any attention?* And so some names never make the list or are quickly removed because of false assumptions. Go on and kick your assumptions to the curb and make a list. Then set up an appointment and ask them if they would be willing to spend a measurable amount of time pouring into someone who wants to maximize their leadership potential. They may give you a cup of coffee each week, they may meet you for a long breakfast or lunch once a month, or they may ask you to shadow them as they pursue a certain project. The point is, you never know until you ask! So make a list, get an appointment, and properly ask. What is the worst that can happen?

PHASE #3: WATCHING AND WORSHIPPING IN THE CHURCH HOUSE

This event in Exodus 33:7–11 designates a phase in Moses and Joshua's relationship because it follows a significant event in the life of Israel. While Moses and Joshua were up on Mount Sinai receiving God's law (Exodus 25–31), the nation of Israel, despite having experienced God's provision and mercy many times before, pleaded with Aaron to make a god for them to worship. So Aaron responded by building a golden calf (Exodus 32). Old Testament scholars believe this was a test for Israel to prove her confidence and faith in Jehovah and his servant Moses (19:9), but instead it gave way to the temptation of flesh and blood.[17]

God demonstrated merciful patience by meeting with Moses in a tent, or tabernacle, of meeting outside the camp. When Moses entered into the tent, a cloud descended upon it symbolizing God's divine presence. The location of this tabernacle of meeting is significant because God had promised a special blessing that he would dwell among his people. But now the presence of God was separated from the encampment as "a sign of the divorce between God and the Israelites."[18] Thus the people of Israel could only observe from the entrance of their own tent as Moses met with the Lord. While Moses was in the tent, each man could only worship from a distance: "All the people saw the pillar of cloud standing at the tabernacle door, and all the people rose and worshipped, each man in his tent door" (Exodus 33:10 NKJV).

While in the tabernacle, "the LORD spoke to Moses face to face, as a man speaks to his friend" (33:11 NKJV). This meeting and subsequent conversation would distinguish Moses from the other prophets, as seen in God's statements when addressing Aaron and Miriam in Numbers 12:6–8.

Scripture continues, "And he would return to the camp, but his servant Joshua the son of Nun, a young man, did not depart from the tabernacle" (Exodus 33:11b NKJV). This is not to say that Joshua was inside the tabernacle, as most scholars do not believe he ascended as far up Mount Sinai as Moses; rather, it demonstrates he was entrusted to be closer to Moses' experience with God's revelation than anyone else in Israel. Additionally, he was given some measure of responsibility in that he stayed behind while Moses returned to camp.

The access and responsibility given to Joshua as he accompanied Moses to the tabernacle and also cared for it are important in understanding Joshua's leadership development. Through this phase of development, we can conclude that Moses was teaching

Joshua how to obey God. Think about it. Joshua was afforded a backstage pass to one of the most important figures in all of human history. While everyone else watched from a distance, Joshua received an up-close-and-personal view of Moses listening, conversing, and worshipping God. We can also make two conclusions concerning our modern-day understanding about the leadership journey:

- People desire to be led, though they don't always make the right decision concerning the type of leader to follow.
- As the mentor-and-emerging-leader relationship progresses and deepens, the weight of responsibility will grow heavier.

It is essential to choose mentors who are imitable, meaning they are an example that can be followed. Moses served that role for Joshua, which is why Joshua was able to care for the church house and be the only witness to what happened in the temporary tabernacle. While there are so many different layers to this event, I think at the end of the day, an obvious conclusion is to choose your mentor well and make sure that person is someone you can follow in word and deed.

Mealtime in our home is for more than just consuming food and fueling the body. We also use this time to have important conversations and family devotions, or to laugh and play games like "Would You Rather . . . ?" A couple of years ago, the family was enjoying a meal and I was leading our devotion. This particular evening we were trying to memorize a short passage of Scripture and then apply it to make-believe scenarios. My then-five-year-old little girl Charis was sitting directly to my right, and upon hearing the verse read aloud, she proceeded to quote the entire thing back to me. I was both surprised and excited, and what happened next forever proves that I am a child of the nineties.

I lifted my hands in the air with victorious celebration, opened my mouth, and shouted, "BOOMSHAKALAKA!" The awkward silence that immediately followed was soon interrupted by Charis's little eyes welling up with tears and the sound of a soft whimper coming from her seat at the table. My wife gave me the kind of look that said, "Are you crazy? Your daughter thinks you just yelled at her in a foreign language because she quoted scripture at the dinner table!" Then she proceeded to explain to Charis that Daddy was actually celebrating and proud that she quoted the verse correctly, and "boomshakalaka" was actually a word he used when he was a kid. I reinforced my wife's words, and we put the whole thing behind us. That is . . . until we went to church the next Sunday.

It seemed like it was going to be your average Sunday when we dropped off our kids for their activities and proceeded to "big church." After the service we went to pick up the kids, and the sweet elderly lady who has been working with children for over forty years was there to greet us. She looked a bit frazzled as we approached the pickup desk. She had a weird look in her eyes and strands of hair misplaced in every direction.

Once we were close enough for conversation, I asked, "So, how were the kids today?" Every parent asks this question just to be polite, but we really don't want to know the answer.

The veteran children's worker looked back at us and said with a confused, exhausted voice, "Everything was okay for a while.

I told the Bible story like I always do, then we formed a circle with the chairs and each child was responsible to retell a portion of the story. Then the strangest thing happened. Every time a child accurately retold their portion of the story, Charis stood on her chair and lifted her hands toward the heavens and yelled a strange saying that I dare not repeat!" She paused, took a deep breath, and continued, "I think she may need professional help!"

I found the entire event to be hilarious. To this day, three years later, it is still funny when she occasionally shouts out, "BOOMSHAKALAKA!" The point of my little story is simply this: I only said the word one time, and because of our relationship, she has repeated it, and led others to repeat it as well.

While a mentoring relationship is not the equivalent of a parenting relationship, the "boomshakalaka" idea is still true. We imitate the behavior we observe in those we look up to. A mentor will have a profound impact on you for the rest of your life, so choose one who is imitable. Follow people with whom you become more impressed when you are given access to their life, not less. Select the type of mentor whose life is absent of hypocrisy and contradiction. This type of mentor will build you up and certainly make you better.

PHASE #4: COMMISSIONED TO ANOTHER PLACE

The final phase of the Moses/Joshua relationship focuses on the events of Numbers 13–14 and can be broken down into three sections: (1) choosing and sending the spies to the land of Canaan, (2) the return and report by the spies, and (3) Joshua and Caleb's response to the congregation. That third part is most helpful for our purposes. Much had taken place leading up to Numbers 13, and a casual reading of Scripture yields the feeling that Israel would never enter the promised land because so much unbelief had characterized the people.

God told Moses to choose a leader from each of the twelve tribes who would serve as the reconnaissance team to scout the land of Canaan (Deuteronomy 1:22–23). After forty days, the spies returned and painted a picture of "a bountiful country—a land flowing with milk and honey" (Numbers 13:27 NLT). The spies even brought back fruit to demonstrate how luscious and fertile the land was. But then in verse 28 their language became extremely pessimistic as they talked about fortified cities and giants who dwelled in the land. Even though Caleb said, "Let's go at once to take the land . . . We can certainly conquer it!" (v. 30) the people of Israel only heard the negative report and began weeping and then grumbling.

Exodus 14:5 is certainly not Moses' finest hour, because he and Aaron fell on their faces in submission before the congregation. They caved. Yet as Moses failed before the complaints of men, he succeeded by inspiring Joshua to lead in his place, a forecast of things to come. Joshua and Caleb's testimony demonstrates their courage and reliance upon Jehovah's sufficiency and faithfulness, as well as the success of Moses' approach to developing Joshua as a leader:

> The land we passed through to spy out is an exceedingly good land. If *the LORD* delights in us, then *He* will bring us into this land and give it to us, "a land which flows with milk and honey." Only do not rebel against *the LORD*,

nor fear the people of the land, for they are our bread; their protection has departed from them, and *the LORD is with us*. Do not fear them. (Numbers 14:7–9 NKJV, emphasis added)

The phrase *passing the baton* often describes what takes place in a mentoring relationship. Just as in a relay race, while there is much that leads up to passing the baton, this action takes place in an instant. Deuteronomy 34:9 is that moment in Moses and Joshua's relationship: "Now Joshua the son of Nun was full of the spirit of wisdom, for Moses had laid his hands on him; so the children of Israel heeded him, and did as the LORD had commanded Moses" (NKJV).

Moses' success in developing Joshua to be a leader was magnified in light of his present failure as one. Therefore, we are provided a picture of a leader in Joshua, who could think independently and critically and make decisions about the present circumstances. This event provides for us two more conclusions concerning the leadership journey:

- The community, and at times even the mentor, is not always right, and there will come a day when the emerging leader must stand alone on his or her own convictions.
- Courage means always doing what is right and trusting God with the results.

The goal of a guide or mentor is to equip the developing leader so that he or she can one day have the capacity to lead independently. This does not mean we do not still go back to our mentors for wisdom; it simply means that we are now equipped to pursue a vision for something God wants. Whether in the valley, on the mountain, inside the church house, or in a foreign land, the trajectory of Joshua's development as a leader had prepared him for the day Moses would no longer be present in his life. A guide who prepares is one who will pray, provide access through relationship, be imitable, and send us out to pursue a vision. The world is very different than it was thousands of years ago, but certain aspects of relationships will always endure. So maybe it's time to put down our all-purpose phones, or quit looking at our watch that has an inferiority complex and wishes it could be the phone, and start experiencing the type of relationship that can catapult our leadership into the future.

BETWEEN TWO WORLDS: THOUGHTS WHILE LEAVING EARTH

Imagine for a moment you are in a room with only a chair, table, keyboard, and computer screen. You've also been told you have twenty minutes to live and the opportunity to write one last message. After the initial panic of imminent death, your attention quickly shifts toward typing. In that moment, the future recipient of your message is probably as important as the content you type. I would write to my wife and children. Some might address a parent or a close friend. Few, I would imagine, would write to a casual acquaintance or strangers. Why? Because when we know our time is limited, we wish to give it to the relationships that matter most to us.

The apostle Paul found himself in a very similar scenario as he was nearing the end of his life. Writing from a prison in Rome, he penned, "For I am already being poured out as a drink offering, and the time of my departure is at hand" (2 Timothy 4:6 NKJV). Paul knew he was dying a slow death in prison, and soon his blood would be spilled like a drink offering, bringing his life on earth to an end. With this knowledge, he put pen to paper with one person on his mind: Timothy, a young man who had been discipled since the age of seventeen by Paul.

Paul's final instruction to Timothy is significant from a leadership development perspective because of the purposeful manner in which Paul was preparing Timothy to lead. With this in mind, the following are Paul's thoughts to young Timothy before leaving planet Earth. To make this chapter exponentially more beneficial, consider this: while Timothy was the direct recipient of this letter, its contents have a much wider yet equally personal audience . . . you. The grand narrative that is the Bible is written to express God's desired will to every reader. Therefore, it is with great confidence that I assure you God's desire is that you maximize your influence. The manner in which that can be accomplished is encompassed in these seven thoughts, from one leader to another, from God to a generation of disciples seeking to lead with grace and courage.

THOUGHT #1: BE ENCOURAGED

Following his greeting at the beginning of 2 Timothy, Paul began his final message with a strong word of encouragement that set the tone for all that would follow. While similar to most of Paul's letters, where the apostle moves from a salutation to an expression of thanksgiving and/or encouragement, his words here took on a more personal nature.[19] New Testament scholar R. C. H. Lenski saw this as demonstrating the personal nature of the letter, calling it "parental" and "inspiring."[20]

First, Paul encouraged Timothy by telling him that he had been constantly praying for him: "I remember you constantly in my prayers night and day" (1:3). This use of hyperbole demonstrates that this letter is more personal and intimate in nature.[21] Paul showed that he was unceasingly mindful of young Timothy with the phrase "night and day." One can only imagine how encouraging it must have been for Timothy to have Paul take such an interest in his personal development.

Second, Paul encouraged Timothy by recognizing his emotions and struggles and by joyfully anticipating their next meeting: "As I remember your tears, I long to see you, that I may be filled with joy" (v. 4). The reference to Timothy's tears probably has to do with the occasion of their last parting of ways in Acts 20:38.[22] We need to be careful here not to accuse Timothy of cowardice, the fear of being left alone, or unmanliness. These are to be understood, as one scholar calls them, as "noble tears,"[23] or as an emotional expression of loyalty and love.

Third, Paul encouraged Timothy by recalling his faith and spiritual heritage when he wrote, "I am reminded of your sincere faith, a faith that dwelt first in your grandmother Lois and your mother Eunice and now, I am sure, dwells in you as well" (v. 5). What a gracious thing to write to Timothy! The words "sincere faith" could also be translated "unhypocritical faith." Paul was reminding Timothy of his spiritual heritage, having been raised in a family that unhypocritically served Christ and then successfully passed its faith on to Timothy. Later, Paul also wrote, "Continue in what you have learned and have firmly believed, knowing from whom you learned it and how from childhood you have been acquainted with the sacred writings, which are able to make you wise for salvation through faith in Christ Jesus" (3:14–15). Thus, even though Paul and Timothy were extremely close, it was Paul reminding Timothy of his relationship with Jesus that served as the greatest source of encouragement.

THOUGHT #2: HAVE A CHRISTOCENTRIC ATTITUDE

Following the opening thanksgiving, Paul reminded Timothy that he had been set apart for ministry. It has been suggested that Timothy possibly lacked a strong father figure (Acts 16:1 says that Timothy's father was a Gentile) and may have struggled with confidence when dealing with opponents.[24] Thus, Paul reminded him to "fan into flame the gift of God" (2 Timothy 1:6) or "stir up the gift of God which is in you" (NKJV). The "gift of God" is probably a reference to Timothy's gift for ministry. The gift, or gifts, of God could be understood as that which is necessary to fulfill the calling God has placed on an individual's life. For Timothy, this was pastoral ministry; for others it could mean athletics or artistry or business. The point is that we have been given gifts, and God expects us to stir them up and put them to use.

This appeal from Paul to rekindle his passion for pastoral ministry then led to a significant statement concerning the intended attitude and demeanor of the young leader: "For God gave us a spirit not of fear but of power and love and self-control" (v. 7).

The word *spirit* is talking about one's attitude or demeanor. First, his attitude should not be that of fear or cowardice, which is the result of a sinful inward focus. For example, Paul was about to lose his life, yet that was not his focus. Paul also told Timothy to have the spirit of power in order to overcome obstacles and to be steadfast in any circumstance. Timothy was reminded, too, of the spirit of love (agape). As with the understanding of power, a proper understanding of love is seen as wholly dependent upon Jesus.

Finally, Paul reminded Timothy of his spirit of self-control, which implies self-discipline, sobriety, sound mind, and sound judgment.[25] Self-discipline here refers to having a level or wise head, which provides wise guidance for the use of power and love.[26] Paul understood that no man can lead others until he can first influence himself; therefore, the ability to control or discipline oneself in obedience to the faith is crucial.

If a spirit of fear focuses on self, then a spirit of power, love, and self-control will help us focus on Christ so we can have a Christocentric attitude.

THOUGHT #3: BE UNASHAMED

Following the description of a Christ-centered attitude, the apostle then warned Timothy: "Therefore do not be ashamed of the testimony about our Lord, nor of me his prisoner, but share in suffering for the gospel by the power of God" (2 Timothy 1:8). We need not make the assumption that Timothy was already ashamed and Paul was thus correcting him. Paul realized it might be a future possibility, so he wanted to make sure it never happened.[27] During the time in which Paul was writing this letter (probably within a year of his death in AD 67), being a Christian often meant criticism and persecution.

Paul, a criminal in the eyes of Rome, encouraged Timothy never to become ashamed of the gospel and, in the same breath, not to be ashamed of his spiritual father. Paul, who represents the inescapable suffering we will all face when being loyal to the gospel, would boast of the suffering of Christ on the cross, the only thing that gave his suffering meaning: "But far be it from me to boast except in the cross of our Lord Jesus Christ, by which the world has been crucified to me, and I to the world" (Galatians 6:14).

And the only way we can ever live out our faith unashamedly and be able to share in Christ's suffering is by the power of God. In

2 Timothy 1:9–12, Paul wrote about a call to a life of *holiness* or, as Hebrews 3:1 states, a "heavenly calling."[28] When we comprehend how much the gospel is worth suffering for, then we will fully understand our calling here on earth, as Paul understood his. From a leadership development perspective, Paul called Timothy to make a present decision (do not be ashamed) about circumstances not yet experienced (Timothy's future as a proclaimer of the gospel).

As we journey throughout this life and the process of becoming an effective leader, there will inevitably be circumstances where it is easier to distance ourselves from the gospel message. I heard a story years ago about a teenage girl who had a mother with a disfigured face. As teenagers tend to do, this young lady continually distanced herself from her mother. She would barely speak to her in public, requested to be picked up late from school, and would hardly look into the stands at her cheering mom during soccer games . . . all in an effort to disassociate. One day the mother confronted her daughter about how she was always distant. The daughter expressed the embarrassment that was multiplied because of the severe disfigurement on one side of her mom's face. The mom then made a decision to share a story that had been kept secret from the daughter all her life.

When the daughter was but an infant asleep in her crib, there was a fire in the house that quickly began to rage out of control. Motherly instinct kicked in, and the mom immediately ran to her baby's room, scooped the infant up in her arms, and proceeded to run through the house toward the front door. The front door was already open because the mother had been in the front yard tending to some flowers when the fire alarm sounded. The young mother was running as hard as she could toward the open front door when out of nowhere a smoldering beam swung down from the ceiling and smashed into the mother's face. As she fell to the ground, seeing stars in the process, she had enough of her wits to throw the baby through the front door to the safety of the yard. Upon hearing this story, the teenage girl felt convicted and ashamed that she had been avoiding the very person who had saved her life.

There will never be a time or event or relationship in which the gospel should be avoided. Live unashamed of the scars of Jesus, for his scars saved us and are still saving us today.

THOUGHT #4: PROTECT YOUR BELIEFS

A great friend and mentor of mine named Bill Brown said to me once, "Brent, you may not live what you profess, but you will live what you believe . . . It is inescapable." In verses 13–14, Paul charged Timothy with keeping the right doctrine and told him how the Holy Spirit could help him accomplish this. He was cautioned not to change anything Paul had taught him and to guard the information like a priceless treasure: "Follow the pattern of the sound words that you have heard from me, in the faith and love that are in Christ Jesus. By the Holy Spirit who dwells within us, guard the good deposit entrusted to you." The point of this advice was that Timothy should "hold fast" and "guard" the "sound words" and "good deposit" that Paul had taught him. Paul had just expressed his resolve in verse 12 and was now urging Timothy to continue on with a similar resolve, made possible by the Holy Spirit. To be a leader of substance, that is, someone who is convinced of his or her worldview, then one must be full of belief. Paul was encouraging this young leader to own his convictions by guarding the truth that had been taught him.

Paul was, in one sense, communicating to Timothy that this leadership task would be a lot of hard work when he used the phrases "hold fast" and "guard." What is helpful for this discussion is that in almost every case, the idea of consistently retaining or possessing is evident. Timothy was to guard the "good deposit" that had been entrusted to him. Since the "good deposit" is sound teaching and doctrine, which is to be shared and taught, this charge has a multilayered meaning being both defensive and offensive. Timothy was to protect the sound doctrine from heresy (defensive) while at the same time investing the sound doctrine through preaching and teaching it to others (offensive).

From a leadership perspective, Timothy learned from Paul that holding fast to and guarding the sound teaching that had been entrusted to him would require a strong work ethic. This aspect of leadership development is often overlooked or ignored in contemporary settings. The rich heritage of right belief has been passed down from generation to generation. It is to be protected and preserved, and for good reason. Could you imagine what would happen if we were not diligent in the task of guarding truth? It could have a detrimental effect on our souls, not to mention those we influence. Therefore, the leader must work hard at believing rightly, because the beliefs we protect can have an eternal impact. We protect the truth to preserve the message so others may, because of the gospel, discover life's purpose.

Before moving on to a different aspect of leadership development in 2 Timothy, attention needs to be given to Paul's comment in 1:15: "You are aware that all who are in Asia turned away from me." On the heels of "holding fast" and "guarding" comes a sober warning to young Timothy: there may be times when the leader has to stand alone. J. Oswald Sanders wrote about loneliness in *Spiritual Leadership*, describing a particular loneliness associated with the life of a leader because he must always be ahead of his followers.[29] He described, "Gregarious Paul was a lonely man, misunderstood by friends, misrepresented by enemies, deserted by converts. How poignant are these words to Timothy."[30]

THOUGHT # 5: RUN AWAY . . . CHASE AFTER

Paul wanted Timothy to be a noble vessel that could be used to honor God and would be prepared to do good work. In an effort to understand the heart of Paul's message to Timothy in the latter part of chapter 2, let's look at verse 22: "So flee youthful passions and pursue righteousness, faith, love, and peace, along with those who call on the Lord from a pure heart." There are two essentials if we want to be individuals "who call on the Lord from a pure heart": *flee* and *pursue*.

First, Timothy was to flee youthful passions. *To flee* carries the meaning of running away (Matthew 24:16; Hebrews 12:25); to escape, avoid danger (Hebrews 11:34); disappear quickly (Revelation 16:20); avoid, elude (1 Corinthians 6:18; 2 Timothy 2:22); or become invisible (Revelation 16:20).[31] The phrase "youthful passions" carries a broader meaning because it doesn't simply refer to sexual lusts but to expressions of youthful immaturity. New Testament scholar Andreas Köstenberger agreed with a broader interpretation of this phrase and used the positive traits as an indication of what to flee: "all unrighteousness (i.e., any form of immorality, including sexual sins . . . and the desire to get rich . . .), lack of faith (including self-reliance in conduct or teaching), lovelessness (and the selfishness that is characteristic of the false

49

teachers), and restlessness (often characteristic of youth)."[32] Paul wanted to make sure that Timothy did not give in to the desire for power, fame, fortune, or worldly satisfaction of any kind.

Second, Timothy was to pursue *righteousness* (meaning moral uprightness), *faith* (meaning trust in God), *love* (meaning a charitable disposition toward others), and *peace* (meaning harmony rather than argumentativeness).[33] The idea Paul wanted to communicate is to continually run away from immorality by chasing after righteousness. "Running away" and "chasing after" are in fact one action. By running away from youthful desires one is running toward holiness.

It can be concluded, then, that viewing this text from a leadership development perspective, Timothy's focus was to be on that which made for holy living. This was to be accomplished by pursuing righteousness, faith, love, and peace within the context of a community of Christ followers. In pursuing these things, Timothy would be fleeing youthful desires.

I had a lot of jobs throughout my teens and early twenties. I have been a custodian, worked landscaping, delivered newspapers, loaded trucks for a shipping company, waited tables, been on a kitchen staff at a barbeque restaurant, worked as a security guard at a juvenile delinquent facility, and the list could go on and on. But one of the most difficult jobs I ever had was a two-year stint working on a lumberyard. And believe me, it was an eye-opening experience for a sixteen-year-old who had been raised in a good Christian home. The lumberyard was in many ways a melting pot; one day you would be working next to a war veteran, and the next day, an ex-con. Because of the diversity, yard foremen would often feel the need to rule with a heavy hand. I will never forget one particular foreman who always began his daily speech with the following, albeit edited, statement, "Men, each of you are only one step away from stupid . . . Don't take that step today and we'll all be okay."

The youthful passions Paul was referring to are simply the immature or stupid decisions we all could potentially make when we are young. That is not to say that leaders with their youthful years behind them do not make stupid decisions; in fact, in this social media age, it seems more and more seasoned influencers have been guilty of this. But Paul was trying to help Timothy establish the healthy habit of avoiding such pitfalls early on so that he would have a reputation for godly behavior. People are much more apt to remember our mistakes than our successes in life; it's just human nature. So live and grow in your leadership with the mentality to flee from sin and chase after righteousness. After all, at any given moment, we are all just one step away from stupid.

THOUGHT #6: THE IMPACT OF "GOD HAS SPOKEN TO US"

In 2 Timothy 3:14–17, the theme of godly living is continued as Paul instructed Timothy to "continue in what you have learned and have firmly believed . . . how from childhood you have been acquainted with the sacred writings . . ." (RSV). As was done in his opening remarks, Paul encouraged Timothy by crediting his spiritual heritage. The role of the Scriptures is also evident here in "making one wise for salvation." The written word illuminates our hearts and minds to the living word, which is Jesus. But the Scriptures profit us with more than just making one wise to salvation; they also serve the purpose of instructing how we should then live. Soon Paul would be dead, and with him any future chance of speaking into Timothy's life. But Timothy did not need to worry, for the voice and message of Scripture would always be available to him.

Verses 16–17 serve as one of the more helpful and insightful texts on the purpose of the Bible both in Timothy's life and for all Christ followers. First, Paul wrote that all Scripture is "God-breathed" or "breathed out by God." The primary purpose of this phrase is so we will know that all Scripture proceeds from God[34] and is also "profitable," meaning beneficial, pertaining to value, usefulness, and profitability (1 Timothy 4:8; 2 Timothy 3:16; Titus 3:8).[35] In short, Scripture, all of which originated with and proceeded from God, is meant to have great value and usefulness in our lives. It is at this point that Paul articulated five ways Scripture impacts a Christian's life:

- "for teaching"—This simply suggests Scripture is a positive source of doctrine.
- "for reproof" (rebuking)—Reproof is not pointing out error simply for the sake of demonstrating error, or as Scottish theologian William Barclay put it: "It is not meant that the Scriptures are valuable for *finding fault*; what is meant is that they are valuable for convincing a man of the error of his ways and for pointing him on the right path."[36]
- "for correction" (restoration)—This is the only time this word is used in the entire New Testament, and it "suggests that Scripture helps individuals to restore their doctrine or personal practice to a right state before God.

Correction is one means God uses in order to restore people to spiritual positions they have forfeited."[37] In other words, Scripture accomplishes more than revealing fault; it also shows the way one can be restored to a right relationship with God.

- "for training in righteousness"—Scholars point out that this phrase is forensic: "that quality which has God's own favor in its verdict, which he as the Judge approves by his verdict."[38] Only the inspired Word of God can educate one in such a way as to secure a favorable verdict with God.

- "that the man of God may be complete, equipped for every good work"—One of the major themes of the Pastoral Epistles is good works (1 Timothy 2:10; 3:1; 5:10, 25; 6:18; 2 Timothy 2:21; Titus 1:16; 2:7, 14; 3:1, 8, 14).[39] The idea of verse 17 is to be prepared for all of life's pursuits, and thus be ready to do good works.

Though there is no way to know, it is an interesting thought experiment to consider if Paul had already been executed by the time Timothy received this letter. If so, this section of the letter would have given him some very real understanding and, in some way, comfort when thinking through the impact of Scripture on his life as he moved into a future leadership role of succeeding Paul. Verse 17 may have offered particular comfort when dealing with an apprehension and uncertainty about the next stage in life. In essence, Paul was telling the young leader that he may not know the future, but the Bible is sufficient in preparing him for anything worth pursuing in the future.

THOUGHT #7: STAY ENGAGED IN THE MISSION . . . KEEP SHARING THE MESSAGE

One final aspect of evaluating 2 Timothy from a leadership development perspective can be seen in 4:2, where Paul wrote, "Preach the word; be ready in season and out of season; reprove, rebuke, and exhort, with complete patience and teaching." There are five essentials in this one verse that begin Paul's final charge to Timothy: "preach," "be prepared/ready," "reprove/correct," "rebuke," and "exhort/encourage." And all of this was to be done with great "patience and teaching." Correcting and rebuking could only be accomplished carefully and with patience so as not to appear to be an angry or dictator-like leader. He was to communicate truth about difficult subjects not with great pride but with humility.

It is easy to look at this final thought and think it does not pertain to us. After all, Timothy was a pastor who preached, and "preach the word" applied directly to his vocation. Many of us will have vocations that do not require us to preach in the traditional sense. But there is an application to be made to the leadership development process that much of 2 Timothy is speaking into. In the end Paul was encouraging Timothy with a sacred sense of urgency to stay engaged in the mission and keep sharing the message of hope in Jesus. One cannot live a life full of sacred intent without being explicit concerning the sacred message. I believe that Paul's final words before leaving planet Earth should inspire every Christian to be categorically clear with our mission and message.

In conclusion, I would like to summarize what we have learned or gleaned from, arguably, history's greatest leader . . . well, besides

Jesus. Some of the characteristics below are embodied in Paul himself, while others are gleaned from his instruction to Timothy. Because this chapter has sought to survey the landscape of an entire book of the Bible, which was a final declaration from one leader to another, the following is an attempt to encapsulate what has been studied about leadership principles:

- The leader should serve as a source of encouragement by praying for, empathizing with, and redirecting focus of those they lead back to their spiritual heritage and personal relationship with Jesus (2 Timothy 1:3–5; 2:1–7; 4:2).
- The leader is to demonstrate a Christocentric attitude characterized by power, love, and self-discipline (1:7).
- The leader is to demonstrate future-tense thinking by anticipating the best in people. A leader is to hold out hope that those being led will observe the call never to be ashamed of the gospel nor of those who suffer on behalf of the gospel (1:8).
- The leader is to be an individual with a high work ethic demonstrating a great resolve and consistency with right doctrine (1:13–14; 3:14–17; 4:2).
- The leader should be prepared to experience a particular type of loneliness that could result from being ahead of the followers or, at times, abandoned by the followers (1:15).
- The leader should have the ability to communicate tough realities and, in the same conversation, be capable of accentuating the positive (1:15–18).

- A leader is to take the initiative to run away from anything that doesn't contribute to righteousness, doesn't build one's faith, can't be done in love, or causes restlessness. A leader should pursue holy living within the context of a community of devoted followers of Christ (2:22).
- The leader is to live aware that one's purpose can only be understood and lived out when pursued within the reality, and by the impact, of Scripture (3:14–16).
- Leaders are to take great comfort in realizing that even though they can't know the future, they can be prepared for it (3:17).
- The leader should deeply value preparation, realizing it is essential for longevity in leading (4:2).
- The leader's message should be characterized by both boldness and patience (4:2).

This chapter has only begun to scratch the surface as we sought to glean how Paul was continuing to prepare and invest in Timothy to lead following his death. That Paul would write his final message before dying to a leader he had personally developed for so many years demonstrates that leadership development was of the utmost importance to Paul. In one sense, we are all between two worlds as we make our pilgrimage toward heaven. The knowledge that Paul would soon see Jesus face-to-face, coupled with the inspiration of the Holy Spirit, provides all who seek it a crystal-clear roadmap to leadership.

TUESDAY

TIME

INTRODUCTION

COSTLY GRACE AND A FAUSTIAN BARGAIN

CHAPTER FOUR

**TIME UNDERSTOOD:
STORIES WITHIN THE STORY**

CHAPTER FIVE

**TIME PURPOSED:
LIVING LIFE'S LAST CIGARETTE**

CHAPTER SIX

**TIME MANAGED:
REDEEMING THE TIME**

COSTLY GRACE AND
A FAUSTIAN BARGAIN

Doctor Faustus is one of the most enduring legends in Western folklore and literature. It is a classic tale of a German scholar who was well versed in theology, philosophy, medicine, and law. Faustus was brilliant, and he consumed information throughout his education with such veracity that he could even outdebate his professors.[1] The story, written in the form of a play by Christopher Marlowe, opens with a frustrated Faustus in his study surrounded by his books. He is displeased because he feels he has learned all he could from subjects having to do with traditional forms of knowledge. In his insatiable desire to learn and know more, he turns to the dark art of magic, which will give him the ability to summon devils.

Faustus is then able to summon Mephistopheles, an unhappy spirit who conspired with Lucifer against God and is now forever damned. He petitions Mephistopheles to return to Lucifer with the following bargain:

> Seeing Faustus hath incurred eternal death
> By desperate thoughts against Jove's deity,
> Say he surrenders up to him his soul

So he will spare him four and twenty years,
Letting him live in all voluptuousness
Having thee ever to attend on me,
To give me whatsoever I shall ask,
To tell me whatsoever I demand . . .[2]

Keep in mind that Marlowe was a contemporary of Shakespeare, and this play was written and published in the early 1590s. All this to say that the verbiage he uses and the style of his writing is a little bit like the 1611 King James Version on steroids. Therefore, let me interpret the above scene to the best of my ability. Faustus sells his soul to Lucifer in return for twenty-four years of Mephistopheles serving his every beckon and wish. Lucifer agrees to the deal, and Faustus is granted his devil-genie. Much of the play follows Faustus's misadventures as he explores the world with his newly bargained-for powers. Doctor Faustus is fearful and full of regret the night before the conclusion of the twenty-four years.

Marlowe writes of Faustus's final hours in such a way that his angst, regret, and fear seem to leap off the page and fill the room. Yet it is too late, and Faustus cannot be saved. He made a deal with the devil and Lucifer is going to collect. Faustus watches the clock, counting the minutes and knowing that when it strikes midnight all is lost for eternity. At one point Faustus cries out,

Now hast thou but one bare hour to live
And then thou must be damned perpetually.
Stand still, you ever-moving spheres of Heaven
That time may cease and midnight never come . . .
O half the hour has passed! 'Twill all be passed anon!

O God,
If thou wilt not have mercy on my soul,
Yet for Christ's sake, whose blood hath ransomed me,
Impose some end to my incessant pain!
Let Faustus live in hell a thousand years,
A hundred thousand, and at last be saved![3]

As you can imagine, Faustus's pleas are not heard, and Lucifer's devils drag him to hell at midnight. The end of the story is a lot like the beginning. Faustus is still trying to bargain for his soul with powers beyond his control.

I have been a Christian for a long time, and I think we often treat time, which is a gift and demonstration of God's grace, like a deal with the devil. We live however we want, using time as a discretionary thing, because in the end we will go to heaven. I know I have been guilty of "eating, drinking, and being merry because tomorrow God will forgive me." Now, I never said those words, but I certainly have communicated such with my actions.

A failure to be intentional with my time is to make grace into something cheap and easy. The story of Doctor Faustus making a deal with the devil has produced the phrase *Faustian bargain* to describe when someone agrees to something bad in order to gain money, success, or power. I think sometimes we treat our faith like a Faustian bargain with a mind-set that says, "I've sold my soul to God. I only have a limited amount of time here on earth, so I will do what I want with my time and periodically pay tribute to God, and then go to heaven when I die." The fallacy of a Faustian bargain is that when it comes to Christianity, faith cannot be reduced to a deal between mere men and God. Redemption from our sins is God's idea and God's initiative. How we use our time is a reflection of our understanding, or misunderstanding, of God's purpose for our lives. God will not be treated like the devil, he will not be bargained with, and grace is not cheap. German theologian Dietrich Bonhoeffer wrote this concerning the difference between cheap and costly grace:

> Cheap grace means grace as bargain-basement goods, cut-rate forgiveness, cut-rate comfort, cut-rate sacrament; grace as the church's inexhaustible pantry, from which it is doled out by careless hands without hesitation or limit. It is grace without a price, without costs.[4]

Of costly grace he wrote,

> Costly grace is the gospel which must be sought again and again, the gift which has to be asked for, the door at which one has to knock. It is costly, because it calls to discipleship; it is grace, because it calls us to follow *Jesus Christ*. It is costly, because it costs people their lives; it is grace, because it thereby makes them live. It is costly, because it condemns sin; it is grace, because it justifies the sinner. Above all, grace is costly, because it was costly to God, because it costs God the life of God's Son—"you were bought with a price"—and because nothing can be cheap to us which is costly to God.[5]

Tuesday is a great day to deal with time. In the beginning, before sin ever entered the world, Adam and Eve were meant to live forever. The fall of mankind changed a lot of things, but chief among them was that death would now be the conclusion of life as we know it. Therefore, Tuesday is a great day to recognize that time is limited and should thus be stewarded. In this section we will explore the concept of time and then how to use and manage it for the glory of God.

CHAPTER FOUR

TIME UNDERSTOOD: STORIES WITHIN THE STORY

In order for us to sacredly use our time, we must first understand the concept of time itself. Simply put, the dictionary defines it as

> *a*: the measured or measurable period during which an action, process, or condition exists or continues: duration
> *b*: a nonspatial continuum that is measured in terms of events which succeed one another from past through present to future
> *c*: leisure <*time* for reading>[6]

But this definition, as helpful as it may be, is lacking the residue of design and purpose that can only be granted by the Creator. We are going to investigate time from a biblical perspective, which will allow us to frame a workable definition, adjust our attitude toward it, and learn to manage it well.

TIME IS THE PRODUCT OF GOD'S CREATIVE ENERGY

Time is something we use to measure everything else. Every event you can think of has been processed through your brain based on your mental map and model of how time works. Time measures the history of the world and all its events. Whether you believe in a literal six-day creation or that the age of the earth is thousands versus millions of years old, it is all processed through a measure of time. Time measures the tenure of countries and nation-states. For example, as I am writing this, the country of my birth is 229 years old, which is nothing compared to the world's oldest country of San Marino founded on September 3, 301. Or consider that the first dynasty recorded in China's history occurred over 3,500 years ago. Comparatively, the United States is just "knee-high to a grasshopper," to use an old phrase that finds its origin in 1814.[7]

Time also measures the event or story that is our life, from beginning to end. When people die there are always two things on their tombstone: the person's name and the person's time on earth. Time is used to process all of the events that occur within one's life story. We use it to mark special occasions such as first communions, graduations, weddings, and anniversaries. We use it even when there is a more constant measuring tool available. For instance, we often use time to measure distance as opposed to miles or kilometers: "I'm about fifteen minutes away" or "I'll be home at six o'clock." Rarely would we make statements like, "I'm four-point-seven miles out and will arrive when I'm zero miles away." Even when I use my phone's navigation ability I always look at the estimated time of arrival instead of the distance. Presidents serve four-year terms; the Winter or Summer Olympics occur every four years; sport seasons last designated amounts of weeks and months; pregnancies are divided into terms, each lasting three months; and the list could go on and on. All events are measured in time.

Because time is created, it is sacred and should be approached with a sacred intent. Theologian Wayne Grudem wrote concerning time:

Before God made the universe, there was no matter, but then he created all things (Gen. 1:1; John 1:3; 1 Cor. 8:6; Col. 1:16; Heb. 1:2). The study of physics tells us that matter and time and space must all occur together: if there is no matter, there can be no space or time either. Thus, before God created the universe, there was no "time," at least not in the sense of a succession of moments one after another. Therefore, when God created the universe, he also created time. When God began to create the universe, time began, and there began to be a succession of moments and events one after another.[8]

Time was created to be a succession of moments and events. It can be dispensed but never regained. And the reason for this is simply that God created it that way. And because God created time, he is not contained by time. He has the capacity to exist above time and look down upon it, viewing its beginning, end, and all the comings and goings in between. As C. S. Lewis wrote in *Miracles*, "To Him all the physical events and all the human acts are present in an eternal Now."[9]

Furthermore, if time was created and its tenure has existed entirely in God's presence, then it is safe to conclude that God is always present. And while his presence is manifested to humans in different ways, for our purposes God is always present because God created time. Thus, the ever-presence of God should fuel the sacred intent of our lives. We should care deeply about the gift of time because our story exists in a much larger story known as history. And though it may sound a bit corny and cliché, because we understand time as created by God, history is really *his*-story.

I spend a lot of time on airplanes, and after a million miles at thirty thousand feet, I am still inspired by the scenes displayed outside my window. The clouds stretching as far as the eye can see look like cotton candy in the sky illuminated by the last bit of daylight. The ocean, which at times looks so smooth and glass-like, feels as if it were taken out of a story about another world. I've flown over certain African countries and almost become hypnotized peering down upon thousands of miles of landscape undisturbed by anything man-made. I cannot help but agree with the words of the psalmist, who never flew in an airplane: "The earth is the LORD's and the fullness thereof, the world and those who dwell therein, for he has founded it upon the seas and established it upon the rivers" (Psalm 24:1–2).

Equally as fascinating is the view of a major city as the plane ascends or descends on approach for landing. The best way I can describe it is to compare it to looking down on an anthill that has been disturbed.

What does this have to do with time as a created thing? It is as if God is above the city with a view of the entire picture and at ground level for millions upon millions of conversations all at the same time. God is not contained by his creation, but is always present in his creation. He can see the entire puzzle before it is pieced together and simultaneously can give his attention to each puzzle piece.

TIME IS A "WISP OF FOG"

God created time as a succession of measurable moments, and he can see the entirety of it. The amount of it granted to each individual is relatively limited. This life is just a thread in a much larger tapestry, a fragment of a full manuscript, and a small piece of clay from a masterpiece sculpture. Eugene Peterson in his paraphrase of the Bible described life this way: "You're nothing but a wisp of fog, catching a brief bit of sun before disappearing. Instead, make it a habit to say, 'If the Master wills it and we're still alive, we'll do this or that'" (James 4:14–15 MSG). The same verses in the *New Living Translation* read, "How do you know what your life will be like tomorrow? Your life is like the morning fog—it's here a little while, then it's gone. What you ought to say is, 'If the Lord wants us to, we will live and do this or that.'"

All of this may seem a bit depressing at first glance, but there is a larger picture to be understood. While we were created to exist in this life and are contained by time, the time granted us is not even close to being the full story. Think of life as simply the opening note of a beautiful symphony or the title page to a great novel, both of which will never come to a completion. For while this present life exists in time, there will be a day when it will come to an end and eternity will begin. The full measure of your story is something that cannot be fathomed by those contained momentarily in time.

It is with this idea that C. S. Lewis concluded the Chronicles of Narnia, in *The Last Battle's* final chapter, "Farewell to the Shadowlands." In the final scene Peter, Edmund, and Lucy are afraid of being sent back to their world once again. Aslan says there should be no fear of that happening since life has ceased for them in the Shadowlands, and then Lewis concludes by stating:

And as He spoke He no longer looked to them like a lion; but the things that began to happen after that were so great and beautiful that I cannot write them. And for us this is the end of all the stories, and we can most truly say that they all lived happily ever after. But for them it was only the beginning of the real story. All their life in this world and all their adventures in Narnia had only been the cover and the title page: now at last they were beginning Chapter One of the Great Story which no one on earth has read: which goes on forever: in which every chapter is better than the one before.[10]

You were created to hope for something that cannot be contained by time. God put eternity in your heart so that a wild hope would arise within you for a world beyond the shadowlands. And once that world is experienced, never again will any of us desire to return to the way things used to be. In heaven there are no "good ol' days"; there is only beauty. And those who are in heaven do not long for earth, but those on earth long for heaven.

With that in mind, James's text makes much greater sense. His phrase "If the Lord wills" provides us with the right attitude to approach time. Likewise, "we will do this or that" demonstrates an intentionality to execute time well. The best way to manage time is to see it as a gift wrapped in grace presented to us with each sunrise. And yet all of the time given is still a brief moment in a much larger story. Therefore, the brevity of life should serve as a motivator to use time well, not because tomorrow we may die, but because tomorrow we may live!

TIME IS THE SOUL'S AUTOBIOGRAPHY

The brief moments that comprise the title page of our eternities are still sufficient to accomplish the tasks of life. How we chose to spend each moment contributes to the narrative that is our lives. Think about it this way: each task, event, and decision that takes place each day of our lives all contribute toward our story. When our story is finally told, there can be but one central theme. I do not know about you, but I want to utilize my time so that redemption is the central theme of my life story. The manner in which we execute our time becomes the autobiography of our soul.[11]

The writer of Ecclesiastes taught that there is a time for everything that needs to be accomplished (3:1–8). The word *time* in this text means an "occasion" or "season" or "purpose" and pinpoints what one wishes to do.[12]

> For everything there is a season, and a time for every
> matter under heaven:
> > a time to be born, and a time to die;
> > a time to plant, and a time to pluck up what is planted;
> > a time to kill, and a time to heal;
> > a time to break down, and a time to build up;
> > a time to weep, and a time to laugh;
> > a time to mourn, and a time to dance;
> > a time to cast away stones, and a time to gather
> >   stones together;
> > a time to embrace, and a time to refrain from embracing;
> > a time to seek, and a time to lose;
> > a time to keep, and a time to cast away;
> > a time to tear, and a time to sew;
> > a time to keep silence, and a time to speak;
> > a time to love, and a time to hate;
> > a time for war, and a time for peace.

As you can see, we are born and we die, and there is a time for all that happens in between whether it be our emotions, relationships, responsibilities, or ambitions. So it is safe to conclude that we manage our time but do not control our destinies. For the Christian, time management is an attempt to saturate all the activities of life with divine purpose by making sure our activities are consistent with God's season for them.

The manner in which we spend our time becomes the manuscript that is our soul's autobiography. In other words, we use time to tell our stories. The goal must then become to proactively ensure that the right emotion, relationship, responsibility, or ambition is happening at the right time. Obedience can be understood as utilizing a succession of measurable moments to bring about success with the right task. When our life is all said and done, we will give an explanation for the use of our time (Matthew 12:36). In the end, which is really the beginning, our use of time will be the ink on the page that is our story or autobiography . . . or rather, the preface to a much greater story that will be lived out in heaven.

CHAPTER FIVE

TIME PURPOSED: LIVING
LIFE'S LAST CIGARETTE

A s a kid I always liked cowboy movies. I was drawn to the sense of adventure, individualism, action and violence, and the added perk of riding a horse and carrying a six-shooter! Cowboys were tough and gritty and had little time for trivial things like sharing emotions and settling down. They did not have an address, but the vast landscape of the Wild West was their home. In the seventh grade I even memorized lyrics to a song about cowboys. The chorus begins,

> Should've been a Cowboy, I should've learned to rope and ride
> Wearing my six-shooter, riding my pony on a cattle drive.[13]

One thing I began to notice in most cowboy films was that there was a lot of death. And there was always a long, drawn-out death scene where one cowboy would remove his hat and kneel next to a dying cowboy who had always been inconveniently shot in the gut. In a typical cowboy-movie kind of way, the dying man would issue his last request . . . to have one final smoke. Then, while taking a few last drags, the two cowboys would exchange words and have a poignant moment. The scene was powerful because the men were acting so out of character. They would share heartfelt things that in any other moment would be un-cowboy-like. In those moments, the words of a dying cowboy were calculated with a profound sense of intentionality. He said what mattered most because the present moment was his last.

What if we lived with a "life's last cigarette" kind of mentality? I do not mean having some morbid sense of death forever looming over us. Nor am I suggesting we all take up smoking. But what if we lived each moment on purpose and with purpose? What if we lived not with a sense of desperation but rather with a sense of urgency? I think that is what Paul was getting at in Romans 12:1: "I appeal to you therefore, brothers, by the mercies of God, to present your bodies as a living sacrifice, holy and acceptable to God, which is your spiritual worship." There, hidden in plain sight, is the very reason God has given us a measure of time.

In what is arguably the most important letter Paul ever wrote, he appealed to the reader to make an offering of his or her life in such a way that it could be called a "living sacrifice." The word *living* speaks to the physical life of the believer.[14] When the words *present* and *sacrifice* are used in the same sentence, John Calvin wrote, "He alludes to the Mosaic sacrifices, which were presented at the altar, as it were in the presence of God."[15] So when we put all this together, "present your bodies as a living sacrifice" presents us with an interesting question: How do we live so that we offer our lives to God in a way that's consistent with an Old Testament understanding of sacrifice?

Certainly, when the word *sacrifice* was read aloud to the house church in Rome, many listeners remembered the sacrificial system of the Mosaic Law in which an animal was born and bred for that moment when it would be placed as an offering before a priest. Its lifeblood was drained, placing humankind's sins on a "system of credit" that would one day be paid in full by the True Sacrifice, the blood of Christ. Knowing this word picture, Paul exhorted the listener or reader not to consider sacrifice as death but as a way to live.

To live as a sacrifice, then, is to live with a sacred sense of intentionality because the present moment in life could be our last. It is to live understanding the blessing of the moment, the favor of the present, is a real reminder of God's mercy. We should live in an effort to capture every moment as if it were our last. Early church father John Chrysostom, who was known for his eloquent speech, explained the phrase "living sacrifice" this way:

> How can the body become a sacrifice? Let the eye look on no evil, and it is a sacrifice. Let the tongue utter nothing base, and it is an offering. Let the hand work no sin, and it is a holocaust. But more, this suffices not, but besides we must actively exert ourselves for good; the hand giving alms, the mouth blessing them that curse us, the ear ever at leisure for listening to God.[16] (The word *holocaust* was synonymous with "sacrifice" and Chrysostom was writing thousands of years before the term would be exclusively dedicated to the events leading up to and during WWII.)[17]

Therefore, time management is more about capturing the moments of life as an act of worship than about managing them. Time management is living with an attitude of intentionality, proactively seizing the present moment or day in order to experience a blessed future.

Paul stamped this message as urgent with his opening words, "I urge you," which could have been translated, "I beg of you, please." The reason for Paul's impassioned plea to capture each moment in faithful obedience to God is found in the phrase "by the mercies of God," which are the justification, sanctification, and glorification of the believer discussed throughout the book of Romans.[18] In other words, the mercies of God are that Jesus has saved and made us right and holy before God; he also will allow us to live in the presence of God forever and ever. In light of all that God has done for us, we are to sacredly care for each moment he has granted us. This is the purpose of time that becomes the autobiography of our souls.

Franklin D. Roosevelt's speech the day after the bombing of Pearl Harbor began, "Yesterday, December 7, 1941—a date which will live in infamy—the United States of America was suddenly and deliberately attacked by naval and air forces of the Empire of Japan." The attack on Pearl Harbor, at that point, was the most devastating loss of life the United States had ever experienced in an attack of that kind. Yet in the years following Pearl Harbor, evidence has been discovered of warnings received by U.S. Intelligence of the Japanese intent. In fact, on the morning of the attack, Washington intercepted a message from Japan indicating an attack would occur at 7:30 a.m. Obviously this was a message that needed to be sent on to Pearl Harbor, but the message was sent as "routine" instead of "urgent." Thus the message did not arrive until 11:00 a.m. on December 7. By that time the Japanese had already destroyed almost twenty naval vessels and two hundred planes; more importantly, over two thousand soldiers and sailors had already died in the attack while another thousand were wounded.

The apostle Paul was pleading with us in Romans 12 to live on purpose and with purpose. He chose to stamp this message as "urgent," rather than "routine," because of the intelligence unpacked earlier in Romans that talked about

- our justification: "Therefore, since we have been justified by faith, we have peace with God through our Lord Jesus Christ" (5:1);
- our sanctification: "But now that you have been set free from sin and have become slaves of God, the fruit you get leads to sanctification and its end, eternal life" (6:22); and
- our glorification: "And those whom he predestined he also called, and those whom he called he also justified, and those whom he justified he also glorified" (8:30).

We need to live toward forever by living as if this moment were our last chance to honor God on planet Earth. Desire to live with a sense of urgency in light of the mercies of God. This is the purpose of time.

TIME MANAGED: REDEEMING THE TIME

Time management is really an attempt to manage the tasks of life consistently with the purpose of time as determined by God. As we have seen, the time we have on earth is brief and the mercies of God demand intentionality. So the question becomes, how do we redeem the time we have been given? Maybe another way of stating this is, how do we bridge the gap between the potential, meaning what we want to see happen, and what actually happens? I want to offer a few thoughts that will help you manage your time well.

DEVELOP A SPIRIT OF INTENTIONALITY

Ephesians teaches us to make the best use of the time we have been given, as the apostle Paul wrote, "Look carefully then how you walk, not as unwise but as wise, making the best use of the time, because the days are evil" (5:15–16). The King James Version uses the phrase "redeeming the time." The word *redeem* can be defined as "to buy up." The way it is used in the phrase here means "to buy up for one's self or one's advantage." Greek scholar Kenneth Wuest wrote, "Metaphorically, it means, to make a wise and sacred use of every opportunity for doing good, so that zeal and well-doing are as if it were the purchase-money by which we make the time our own."[19] And there it is, the spirit of intentionality dedicated to making the time our own. So much of time management comes down to becoming passionate about what matters most . . . or maybe what should matter most.

It is our responsibility, in one sense, to own the time we have been given. It is a spiritual thing then to own your schedule as opposed to your schedule owning you. Many of us don't feel we own our schedules but rather we feel like somewhere along the way our time, and with it our lives, were abducted and now we are machines in the matrix, which is carrying out tasks designated for us. It is time to break free from that kind of thinking, and that begins with an attitude.

I am a big believer that one's attitude is directly tied to . . . well, everything we do in life. Pastor Chuck Swindoll wrote in his book *Strengthening Your Grip* the following concerning attitude:

> Words can never adequately convey the incredible impact of our attitude toward life. The longer I live the more convinced I become that life is 10 percent what happens to us and 90 percent how we respond to it. I believe the single most important decision I can make on a day-to-day basis is my choice of attitude. It is more important than my past, my education, my bankroll, my successes or failures, fame or pain, what other people think of me or say about me, my circumstances, or my position. Attitude keeps me going or cripples my progress . . . It alone fuels my fire or assaults my hope. When my attitude is right, there's no

barrier too high, no valley too deep, no dream to extreme, no challenge too great for me.[20]

The Bible speaks of the attitude a Christian should have when Paul writes in 2 Timothy 1:7 that "God gave us a spirit not of fear but of power and love and self-control." The word *spirit* speaks to our disposition and outlook—in other words, our attitude. Fear is not a gift from God. It is contrary to the power of the Holy Spirit within us, which helps us be bold and strong, love so that we can forgive and not seek revenge, and live with self-control so that we may be wise in the use of power and love.[21] Fear occurs when our focus is on tasks and responsibilities, which cause us to wonder, *How will I ever get it all done?* Fear is cowering under the pressures of this world instead of trusting in the gifts God has given us.

The spirit of intentionality keeps us focused on God and the work of the Holy Spirit in us. The great preacher John Wesley, who led the evangelical movement that would become Methodism, followed a rule for living that demonstrates the type of attitude I am describing:

Do all the good you can,
By all the means you can,
In all the ways you can,
In all the places you can,
At all the times you can,
To all the people you can,
As long as ever you can.[22]

SEE YOURSELF AS THE PRODUCER OF YOUR LIFE'S STORY

As you can probably tell by now, I am a huge fan of viewing things through the lens of a story. I believe the Bible is the greatest story, and all others only make sense in light of it. I believe that we are privileged to tell a story with our lives . . . and hopefully we're telling the kind of story others will want to emulate. If your life were a movie, then certainly God would be the director: "I know, O LORD, that the way of man is not in himself, that it is not in man who walks to direct his steps" (Jeremiah 10:23). But I believe that God has tasked us to be the producers of our stories. A film producer does not sit in the director's chair but is still very hands-on with the technical side. For our purposes, let us pretend that because of budgeting restraints, the producer is tasked with making all of the decisions below. If you can view your life through the eyes of a producer, then answering these questions is another step toward redeeming your time.

What Is the Centralized Theme at the Heart of the Story?

Every story has a centralized theme, the one idea that is carried throughout the story. It transcends the story because it is larger than any one story. Of course, the great example of this is the grand narrative of Scripture, which can be understood in four parts: creation, the fall, redemption, and restoration. But if we were to even casually survey the plot, it would become obvious that redemption is the centralized theme. It receives far more airtime than any other part, beginning in Genesis 3:15 with the promise of Jesus. In fact, theologians have referred to the Old Testament as "redemptive history," thus further demonstrating the central theme.

Just as our discussion on leadership began in a very devotional place, so does the management of the moments. Time management must be devotional before it is practical. It must be seen as something sacred before it is accomplished. And all of the comings and goings of our lives will, in the end, produce one clear message. The challenge is to choose what that answer will be now because, as we all know, time cannot be reused or recycled. There are no rollover minutes. So what do you want the central message of your life to be? I hope that redemption is the theme of your story. I hope that if your life were a story observed, Jesus would be at the center of it all. I would go as far as to say that if redemption is not the theme of your story, then your story probably is not worth telling. But if redemption is the theme, then the story is worth telling, retelling, and even imitating.

Who Are the Main Characters and Supporting Cast?

There has never been a person born who preselected his or her family. We did not choose when and how we came into this world. We did not choose our parents, and when we are toddlers or young children, we don't even decide when or what we eat, where we live and go to school, and so on and so on. But for us all there comes a day when we start making those decisions. We begin to pick out our own clothes, determine when or if we will eat breakfast. Many of us select what college or graduate school we'll attend. What person we marry, what job opportunities we prepare for or say yes to. And there is a day when we begin to decide whom we "cast" as the main characters in our story.

A lot of people spend much of their life blaming the past for their present circumstance. And while much of our past could not be controlled, there comes a point when you start determining what the past moments will look like. It is important to remember that your childhood past will not necessarily determine all of your future. The day, week, month, and year you are living in will soon fall into that broad category called your past. President Harry S. Truman had a sign on his desk that read, "The Buck Stops Here!" With much of our future past, the buck will stop with us.

Which brings us to one of the most important decisions you or I can make with our time—who we will spend it with. The person or persons we give the majority of our time to become the main characters in our story. No way around it—that's just how it is. Those who receive less time become the supporting cast, whether they are our friends, our employer, our spouse, or our kids. The weird thing about the age in which we live is someone or even some*thing* very impersonal can become the main character(s) in our story. Some of us spend most of our leisure time living vicariously through someone else via social media. Others are addicted to a video game in which they partner with someone online, in another state or country, through a player character. In fact, addiction of any kind can become the main character in your story, as can a certain GPA or work accomplished at the office. Those individuals or activities play a significant role in our lives.

What Is the Scene That Needs to Be Accomplished Today?

After we establish the major theme of our life and choose who will be the main characters in our life, we can then focus on what that looks like on a day-to-day basis. If we were to think of each day as a scene, what scenes need to be accomplished and in what order? A helpful way to organize your time each day is to evaluate and prioritize. Obviously some tasks, like diet and exercise, will be daily activities. Some other regular activities may include prayer and Bible study time, school, or work. Once you determine daily tasks and where they fit into your schedule, the next step is to ask this one simple question: "What is the most difficult task I have to accomplish today?" Your calculus homework or that history assignment? Whether (or when) to have that difficult meeting with your boss or coworker? Or finally getting off the couch to go for a run? Whatever the difficult task may be, do it first and get it out of the way! It's amazing how doing the hard things first creates momentum for accomplishing everything else in a more enjoyable manner.

You are the producer of the movie that is your life story. You choose the plot line that demonstrates the central theme, you choose the characters, and you choose how the scenes will be accomplished. Heck, you even get to choose the set design, the soundtrack, and the food. Our time gets away from us when we let other people or other things take charge of it. But it is yours, and you decide how you spend it.

Identifying and focusing on the three most important aspects—theme, characters, and scenes—is pretty simple, to be quite honest with you, so that's why I like it. If my plan has too many steps, it becomes pointless. After all, life is complicated enough! The plan we put in place to organize it shouldn't further complicate the narrative.

LEARN TO CHEAT WELL AND OFTEN

Years ago when Christina and I were newlyweds living in Atlanta, we attended North Point Church under the leadership of Pastor Andy Stanley. On one occasion he delivered a message that resonated with me more than most and has served me well over the last thirteen years of marriage. It was a sermon called "Choosing to Cheat" and eventually became a book under the same title.[23] The central idea of the sermon is that all of us are granted twenty-four hours a day, which doesn't seem like enough time to accomplish all the tasks and responsibilities on our lists. Something is going to get cheated, whether it's homework, time with the kids, a round of golf, another meeting at the office, and the list goes on and on. In other words, many times saying yes to one event or activity automatically means saying no to another. Therefore, since one area of life inevitably affects another, where and how we choose to cheat is a clear demonstration of what we value.

It all comes down to understanding that the measure of time given to us is ours to use, for better or worse. Knowing that you inevitably have to "cheat" something or someone, you must begin by asking who in your life feels cheated. Andy compared it to asking someone to hold a rock for an indefinite amount of time. If you ask me, I might agree to do it, but eventually my physical ability to hold the rock will give out. I will not have the ability to hold the rock anymore, and then the rock will get dropped. It may hit the ground and shatter into a hundred different pieces. When we cheat, we are asking the most important people in our lives to hold a rock they were never intended to hold for longer than they are able to hold it. And the scary thing is that when they drop the rock, sometimes the pieces can't be put back together. So here is your challenge:

First, take an inventory of your time over the next month by asking those who matter most in your life if they feel cheated. This will mean some tough, possibly lengthy, and probably tear-filled conversations.

Second, decide never to cheat time from what matters most in your life (i.e., family and God). Just remember, in doing this you will also be deciding to cheat in other places (hobbies, work, school activities, sports). This will require a willingness to miss what matters less to be present for what matters most. And you may receive less recognition or miss out on certain opportunities. Become comfortable with dedicating your time to what can't be measured in spreadsheets, points on a scoreboard, awards, or dollars earned. Time with family, a spouse, a youth group, or your siblings is difficult to measure because love does not fit on spreadsheets or scoreboards, and it does not come with an award or earn you any money. Love spent and relationships enjoyed are rewards unto themselves, and in the end this matters deeply to us because it is close to God's heart.

Third, ask God to fill in the gaps at the places you are now cheating. It is important to get steps two and three in the right order because obedience is determining the *what* before we understand the *how*. What we will discover in the end is that choosing to cheat is really a decision to trust and obey. Besides, God is able to accomplish infinitely more than we ever could with a million lifetimes.[24]

CONVERTING TIME INTO PRODUCTIVITY

On a much more practical level, how do we convert the time given into productivity toward certain tasks? Converting the time we have into tasks accomplished, simply put, revolves around having a plan. Over the years I have seen and used a wide variety of time-management tools in an effort to help me maximize my time and meet my goals. The evolution of these tools, largely due to technology, has accelerated to the point that now we can customize the way we manage our time.

Years ago I began with a paper planner and a FranklinCovey time management seminar. This was incredibly beneficial and served me well for years. That is, until the explosion of that beautiful technology called a smartphone, and all the apps that came with it. So, in recent years, I have adapted the principles of time management that I learned from FranklinCovey to an application that can be used on my phone, tablet, or laptop. At any rate, you have to discover what works for you. So go ahead and experiment with different plans and mediums. It may be that a paper planner is what works best for you. Or you may need an app. Maybe a combination of both. But at the end of the day, all good time management plans and tools facilitate the following in our lives:

- The ability to manage daily tasks
- The technology to schedule a task for another time
- A reserved space for goal-setting and planning
- A manageable calendaring feature

Find what works for you no matter how long it takes. Because as the oft-quoted Benjamin Franklin said, "If you fail to plan, you are planning to fail!"

USE REGRET IN THE PAST AS MOTIVATION TO REDEEM TIME IN THE FUTURE

All of us have wasted time on activities, or even relationships, that are not beneficial and may even be sinful. Time wasted is like spending money on products only advertised on TV at two o'clock in the morning. A thirty-second commercial may promise to make our car look brand new, our wood furniture appear as if the Amish made it, or our skin look twenty years younger. And all of this usually for $19.95. (But wait, there's more!) Or time wasted is like ordering candy for dinner when you could have had something healthy. Or it can be like reading the *National Enquirer* to get real news. In short, time wasted is pointless.

William Wilberforce was the English politician who became the leader of the movement to abolish the slave trade. He is celebrated as one of the greatest leaders in history. Biographer Kevin Belmonte accurately described him as a hero for humanity.[25] At the age of seventeen, Wilberforce entered St. John's College, and following the death of his grandfather and uncle, and under the guardianship of his mother, he was left an independent fortune.[26] Therefore, with almost unlimited spending capabilities and the evangelical voice and guidance of his aunt and uncle far removed from his life, a young Wilberforce entered college. An unregenerate seventeen-year-old, on his own for the first time, with all the money he could ever want . . . What could go wrong?

On his first night he had supper with his advisor, William Arnald, who in turn introduced William to two undergraduate students. Wilberforce described them as "licentious a set of men as can well be conceived. They drank hard, and their conversation was even worse than their lives. I lived amongst them for some time, though I never relished their society . . . and after the first year I shook off in great measure my connection with them."[27]

In other words, Wilberforce spent the first year at college partying hard. During this time frame he devoted himself to playing cards, singing, drinking, listening to music, and hosting dinners. His friend Gisborne recalled Wilberforce's room being filled with students from the time he woke, which was usually very late, to the time he went to bed, which was also very late.[28] As Belmonte observed, "He was more irresponsible than immoral."[29] Nevertheless, because of his quick intellect and good memory, he would pass his examinations, though as Pollock observed, it would be done "without glory."[30] He would be awarded a BA in 1781 and an MA in 1788.[31]

One of Wilberforce's great regrets in life was the time he squandered at St. John's College. Wilberforce would also regret that his tutor and his colleagues never instructed him on a strong work ethic or on a systematic approach to his studies.[32] In retrospect, Wilberforce commented that his close friends at that time made it their goal "to make and keep me idle."[33] To summarize, he wrote of time wasted, "Whilst my companions were reading hard and attending lectures, card parties and idle amusements consumed my time."[34] Following Wilberforce's conversion to Christianity and his realization that the great objective of his life was the abolition of the slave trade, he became a dedicated steward of his time.

For Wilberforce, time wasted actually became a motivating factor. There is a great lesson to be learned here. Time wasted cannot be relived, but in some measure it can have redeeming benefits if we allow it to continually remind us of what we never want to waste again.

WEDNESDAY

CALLING

INTRODUCTION
STAY IN YOUR OWN LANE

CHAPTER SEVEN
GOING RETRO WITH THE REFORMERS

CHAPTER EIGHT
A HYPOCRITE'S CONFESSION

STAY IN YOUR OWN LANE

"What is God's calling on my life?" A reasonable and common question for all of us to ask ourselves, right? Answering it incorrectly could have dire consequences, if not immediately, then sometime in the future. But if we understand our true calling, life can be rich with purpose. I do not believe that God is playing a game of hide-and-seek with our callings, hiding them inside some kind of vault and hoping we will figure out the code or password to unlock it. I think he makes it clear, as with so many other things, when the Scriptures illuminate our paths.

One encouragement in our search is knowing that greater minds have grappled with calling throughout history. As they discovered, calling stretches across the vast landscape of life's journey. There are no phases of life or decisions we make that will go untouched by calling when it is properly understood. Thus, we will look at four sides of our calling in an effort to understand it better, and then we will turn our attention to practical help that will allow us to pursue it with greater focus and determination.

The other day I was driving down a major interstate where there was a considerable amount of construction. You have probably witnessed a similar scene where it looks like the earth vomited bright orange for about a quarter of a mile. I realize those guys know what they are doing, but it does appear a bit chaotic at times with orange cones, flags, drums, signs, and vests scattered in every direction. Anyway, as I recently approached this scene, one diamond-shaped sign that stood out among the rest read, "Stay in Your Own Lane." My understanding of this is that though the scene may appear a bit chaotic and confusing, if I stay in my lane I am going to be safe and okay. In my lane there will not be anxiety or ambiguity of any kind. An understanding of calling is a lot like staying in our own lane. When we do, we will experience a life free from the entanglements of false expectations and exhaustion.

CHAPTER SEVEN

GOING RETRO WITH THE REFORMERS

B etween the years 1483 and 1546 there lived a man whose impact was so great that it is difficult to measure. During his lifetime he was seen as pure evil by some but theologically correct by many. In the nearly five hundred years since his death, both Catholics and Protestants agree that he positively changed the course of Western history.[1] The man to whom I refer is none other than Martin Luther. He was a monk, priest, and professor, but it was his theological insights inspiring a deep-seated conviction that set him apart as a leader in what is now referred to as the Protestant Reformation, where many departed from the Catholic Church.

Of the many frustrations Luther held with the Catholic Church, one was the selling of indulgences. An *indulgence* is defined as "remission of part or all of the temporal and especially purgatorial punishment that according to Roman Catholicism is due for sins whose eternal punishment has been remitted and whose guilt has been pardoned."[2] Friars and priests sold indulgences, and Luther greatly objected to their use as a means of purchasing forgiveness of sin, whether for one's self or someone who had already died.

This, in part, led him to write his Ninety-Five Theses in 1517, which challenged many of the Catholic Church's views, including the pope's authority. Luther's theological positions taught that salvation could not be earned but rather could be received only by grace through faith, that all Christians are priests, and that the Bible is God's divine source for revealed knowledge to which all have access. His refusal to recant his positions led to his excommunication from the Catholic Church and being labeled an outlaw by the emperor. The Reformation helped start a movement that paved the way for individuals in the body of Christ to think and decide their own convictions. Before Luther, there was one Universal or Catholic Church. In the years since Luther . . . well, you can see for yourself.

One of the truths this theological giant promoted is known as the doctrine of vocation. The word *vocation* comes from the Latin word for "calling," so these terms can be used interchangeably. Since *vocation* may have a perception that the word relates only to one's job or employment, from this point on I will use the word *calling* in reference to Luther's doctrine. Gene Edward Veith, in his book *God at Work*, summarized the doctrine of calling as "a comprehensive doctrine of the Christian life, having to do with faith and sanctification, grace and good works. It is a key to Christian ethics. It shows how Christians can influence their culture. It transfigures ordinary, everyday life with the presence of God."[3] For instance, Veith said this about vocation:

> Instead of seeing vocation as a matter of what we should
> *do*—what we must *do* as a Christian worker or a Christian
> citizen or a Christian parent—Luther emphasizes what

God *does* in and through our vocations. That is to say . . . above all vocation is a matter of Gospel, a manifestation of *God's* action, not our own. In this sense, vocation is not another burden placed upon us, something else to fail at, but a realm in which we can experience God's love and grace, both in blessings we receive from others and in the way God is working through us despite our failures.[4]

Based on this teaching, the Christian life could be understood through a series of callings. We are called to be a part of God's church, build healthy families, be responsible citizens, and pursue a vocation that contributes to culture. In essence, calling is to be viewed as plural (fourfold), not singular. Furthermore, individuals will fulfill multiple roles under the banner of calling.[5] For example, a woman may fulfill the roles of mother and wife within a family. Or a citizen will vote, pay taxes, attend town hall debates, or maybe even run for political office. These callings will continue to make more sense as we better understand how God has created us and then discover the many jobs he has for us. The fourfold approach (church, family, citizenship, and contributor) allows us to simplify how we process our lives, thus affording the ability to see all of life through the lens of calling.

CHURCH

One of the more difficult things to put into words is our calling out of darkness and into the marvelous light that is Jesus. I say this because words are a necessary but weak means by which to communicate that we were dead, lifeless, bound for eternal separation from God and purpose . . . before something unbelievable happened. Maybe it is hard to describe because miracles are so supernatural and words seem so human. To be dead in sin is to be consumed more and more with nothingness. It has been described by some theologians that to sin is to "de-create." Scripture says all that God has created is good (1 Timothy 4:4). Evil, therefore, is not a created thing but rather a perversion of the good that has been created. When we were drowning in the nothingness of separation from God, hope seemed to have gone on vacation, never to return. That God calls us to himself, that he invites us into the marvelous light, is God injecting hope into a, humanly speaking, hopeless situation.

There may be no better example of this in Scripture than the conversion of Saul. Saul was born and raised in Tarsus, which was a chief city in Cilicia, a province of southeast Asia Minor. Its geographical location made it an important city, being protected by the Taurus Mountains and located in a fertile valley along the banks of the Cyndus River, about ten miles from the Mediterranean Sea. Tarsus was also a free city that, because of its location, enjoyed great wealth. It was considered a center for culture, art, and education in the Roman world, rivaling that of Athens and Alexandria.[6] It was in this city that Saul would spend his early years. His father was of the strictest sect of the Jews, a Pharisee, of the tribe of Benjamin, of pure and unmixed Jewish blood (Acts 23:6; Philippians 3:5).[7] Therefore, Saul was a Jew who grew up in a multifaceted Greek culture (Acts 21:39) as a Roman citizen (22:25). The combination of these three influences—the religion and heritage of being a Jew, being born into and educated in a Greek culture, and enjoying Roman citizenship—provided Saul with an open door to most of the known world. He also became a rabbi studying in Jerusalem under a much-respected Pharisee and member of the Sanhedrin named Gamaliel (22:3).

The question then becomes, how did Saul go from a well-educated Jewish rabbi with Roman citizenship to the leader of those persecuting disciples of Jesus? The answer, of course, is found in his conversion and calling. Acts 9 opens by painting a picture of a man out for blood. Three times it is mentioned that he persecuted "both men and women," emphasizing the level of cruelty to which he had turned. He himself stated when testifying to King Agrippa, "I punished them often in every synagogue and compelled them to blaspheme; and being exceedingly enraged against them, I persecuted them even to foreign cities" (Acts 26:11 NKJV). Calvin said, "He raged like an untamed beast" and that, after persecuting the disciples when his hands were "imbued with innocent blood, he proceeded in like cruelty, and was always a furious and bloody enemy to the Church."[8] Saul's actions could be justified because his was a life completely absent of the grace of God and as such led to having innocent blood on his hands. A life devoid of God's grace will always paint a tragic picture. What would be quite beautiful is that after his conversion, *grace* would become the most mentioned word in all his letters.

While on his way to persecute the disciples that were in Damascus, just as he had done in Jerusalem, "suddenly a light from heaven shone around him. And falling to the ground he heard a voice saying to him, 'Saul, Saul, why are you persecuting me?'" (Acts 9:3–4). The wording of this question is of great significance and most likely shaped the outworking of Saul's salvation and ministry. New Testament scholar Lenski commented on the meaning of stating someone's name twice:

One should go through the Scriptures and note these du-
plications: Saul, Saul—Martha, Martha—David's lament
over Absalom, and others. In varying ways they express
an emotion of deepest concern but never anger. Why,
yes why, was Saul persecuting Jesus? This question called
upon Saul to probe his soul in regard to the terrible work
in which he was engaged. To persecute the disciples is to
persecute the Master.[9]

Jesus was not standing there with angry judgment, which
could have been represented by a sword or some other weapon.
His question no doubt led Saul to contemplate his sin and consider
his relationship with God. In that moment, he must have realized
the futility of his own self-righteousness as Jesus was calling Saul
unto himself and to the mission of the church. It is important to
understand that the narrative in Acts 9 is not just the conversion
account of Saul becoming Paul; it is also the calling that would be
his vocational service of missionary, church planter, evangelist, etc.

To understand the calling God was placing on Paul's life, Luke
provided a conversation between a disciple in Damascus named
Ananias and Jesus in Acts 9:10–16. The most relevant part of that
dialogue to the topic of calling comes in verses 15–16 when Jesus
said that Paul "is a chosen instrument of mine to carry my name
before the Gentiles and kings and the children of Israel. For I will
show him how much he must suffer for the sake of my name." The
emphasis on Paul being "chosen" speaks of the divine call, which
set him apart from birth (Galatians 1:15).[10] The word translated
"instrument" is any kind of vessel that could be carried with one's
hands or on one's shoulders.[11] Paul is going to carry the Lord's

name before Gentiles, kings, and the children of Israel. Paul would himself use these terms when illustrating God's sovereignty in election (Romans 9:21–23; 2 Corinthians 4:7; 2 Timothy 2:20–21).[12]

The language used in Acts 9:15–16 is also reminiscent of giving one's testimony in a legal setting. When Jesus spoke of Paul's audience being Gentiles, kings, and the children of Israel, it was a picture of Paul on trial before Gentile rulers like Felix and Festus (chaps. 24–25), in front of kings like Agrippa (chaps. 25–26), before local Jewish synagogues and even the Sanhedrin (chap. 23).[13] Therefore, it was on a road to Damascus attempting to stop the movement of Christianity that Paul was converted to Christianity. Shortly thereafter, while still blinded from the light of heaven, he was filled with the Holy Spirit and told of his future.

The marvelous light offers hope to engage the greatest movement in history, the movement of the church. We are the called ones, everyday priests, chosen by God to carry out his great cause, which is the advancement of the name of Jesus and the church. We focused on this aspect of calling first, and dedicated more time to understanding it, because it predictably affects the other callings in our life. Os Guinness echoed this when he wrote, "Calling is the truth that God calls us to himself so decisively that everything we are, everything we do, and everything we have is invested with a special devotion and dynamism lived out as a response to his summons and service."[14]

FAMILY

God is all-powerful and did not create family because he had run out of options. Think about it. He easily could have spoken an entire world's population into being in one moment, but he did not. Rather, he chose to create one man and one woman who would produce children and populate the world. God's plan for population is families making people. Families make people and people make more families. That means more people experiencing the love between husband and wife, more babies being born, more babies growing up in loving homes, more family vacations and great dinner conversations, more birthday wishes and good-night kisses, more baptisms, and more following Jesus. And, of course, more people reading God into their family relationships translates into more people living a life stamped with calling.

There are three roles within the family dynamic that need to be understood: spouse, parent, and child. First, let's take a brief look at the role of spouse and the marriage relationship. Marriage is to be a lifelong covenant relationship between a man and a woman, as it was established by God in creation. The nucleus of the marriage relationship is covenant love that creates a basis for stability in marriage and society.[15] All romance, friendship, sexual desires, and activity should be filtered through the holy commitment that is the heartbeat of the relationship. Marriage is the arena through which we fulfill God's mandate in Genesis to "become one flesh" and "be fruitful and multiply." Therefore, we must view marriage through the lens of calling. You and I are called to marry well and in so doing fulfill God's purposes. In fact, God's math is quite peculiar when it comes to marriage: one flesh + one flesh = united into one. Furthermore, the marriage relationship should grow sweeter with time as it marinates in covenant love.

And, as to be expected, all of this "becoming one" will lead to fruit, that being children. Psalm 127:3 teaches, "Children are a gift from the LORD; they are a reward from him" (NLT). So all of us were a gift and blessing to someone whether we were anticipated, wanted, or even rejected. As our parents' gift, we are to honor them according to Exodus 20:12. What does it mean to honor one's parents? The word *honor* could also be translated "glorify" and is used elsewhere to refer to God's relationship with his people as father.[16] The command to honor our parents is in no way a call to worship or idolize them. Instead, this text demonstrates that because of the authority granted to parents, they deserve authority and respect like we would give to God. So children are a gift and reward from God, and in turn those children are to honor and respect their parents. The challenge for any child, young or old, is to view oneself as a gift. But not just any gift, rather the gift that keeps on giving respect and honor the whole life through.

CITIZENSHIP

So far it all seems very plausible that God has called us to himself and the movement of Christianity and that we are called to make families. But now we will even see that to be a citizen of a nation or country is a divine calling. Again, Veith helps us understand this:

> God works through governments and is hidden in cultural institutions. As such, His moral law *is* binding, even among those who do not know Him, but in whom he still operates . . . Christians do have a vocation to be good citizens, in every way that implies. They are to see God's authority as looming behind the secular authorities who govern their nation.[17]

This is not to say that every decision made by a political leader is right or moral or just, but rather that God's sovereignty includes the public square.

Think about it this way. Let's say that three kids are allowed to go into the backyard and play by their mother. It is that magical time of the day for kids when they get home from school and dinner is still a couple of hours away. They can run and play games in the backyard and have fun like kids should be allowed to do on a regular basis. While those three children are playing in the backyard, they decide to transform part of the swing set into a castle. Immediately, the oldest boy decides he is the king of the castle and begins to rule over the backyard from his perch with the boundaries of his kingdom being a chain-link fence. During his tenure as king of the castle, all the riches and the fame start to go to his head and he starts to act corruptly. He begins to order his younger sister, who is a commoner, to bring him this or to fetch him that. One of his commands is that she get on her hands and knees and collect leaves and then strategically place them around his throne with the other commoner, his younger brother.

At this moment the king has never felt so strong, so in control of his own fate. Little does he know that his mother has been watching out the window as the scene unfolds and is very aware that the younger brother and sister are not enjoying themselves. Soon mom calls everyone inside to get cleaned up for dinner. Not long after dad returns home and the family sits down to enjoy a meal, the medieval drama from the backyard has become a distant memory. After dinner, before one dish from the table is collected and put in the dishwasher, the mother has an announcement: "As the queen of this castle, I declare that for the remainder of the night all commoners shall wear the crown! Those who formerly wore the crown should be their servants and thus clear the table, clean the dishes, and bring those now wearing a crown their desert!" Immediately following the proclamation, the mother pulls out two paper crowns she had made. She then places the crowns on the heads of her two youngest children.

At that moment, the cruel king who formerly sat on his throne is humbled to the role of dishwasher. The queen mother only allows the scene to last long enough to make her point, since she is the ultimate ruler over the backyard and its king. The evening ends with the entire family enjoying each other's company and playing a game around the dinner table in complete equality.

Nations and their governments are powerful things, to be sure. A government can wage a war that brings about the death of tens of thousands of young men and women. On the other hand, a nation can rally around the needs of another and save the lives of tens of thousands. Governments have all kinds of power to save, destroy, protect, and deliver. And yet even America with her superpower status is a little kid wearing a make-believe crown in the backyard compared to God's sovereignty. Government leaders may rule, but they do so in God's backyard and under his authority. Romans 13:1 reads, "Let every person be subject to the governing authorities. For there is no authority except from God, and those that exist have been instituted by God." Depending on the government, nation, and time, the present moment may appear to be outside of God's control, but believe me when I say that God, in all his sovereignty, is the ultimate ruler, and he will make all things right.

Even though we now play in the backyard where everyone

does not always get along or act as they should, one day we will be around the table at a feast compared to no other (and I really hope they don't serve broccoli), and all the pain, tears, and bad stuff from this life will have passed away. As we await the new heaven and new earth, the backyard will have to do, meaning we should submit to authority and the process of government. First Peter 2:13–14 teaches us, "Be subject for the Lord's sake to every human institution, whether it be to the emperor as supreme, or to governors as sent by him to punish those who do evil and to praise those who do good." Since we are in the backyard, we should act a certain way because, after all, it does belong to the real King.

CONTRIBUTOR

Two women wake up in separate households around the same time to the annoying sound of their alarm clocks. Depending on the morning, one or both may hit the snooze button a couple of times before emerging from the fog of slumber. Each woman then proceeds to accomplish something miraculous, walking into her bathroom looking like someone who survived the zombie apocalypse and emerging like a professional woman stepping out of a catalog. Then it is out the door with coffee and bagel in hand and some hybrid briefcase/giant mom purse over their shoulders (I don't know, but it's big and colorful and made from luxurious leather). After a thirty-minute commute, during which the bagel and coffee are consumed without disturbing makeup, both arrive at their places of employment.

One is a graphic designer for a local marketing firm that focuses on unique clientele such as a grocery store specializing in organic food. The other is a third-grade teacher with twenty-two students all coming from different backgrounds. The graphic designer usually gets off work around 4:00 p.m., leaving her enough time to pick up her kid from school and take him to soccer practice twice a week. The schoolteacher is heading home about the same time to reconnect with her husband and three dogs. Both women enjoy their respective jobs most days. Sure, there is the occasional pee-pee accident during recess, or the produce division thinks the celery packaging design is not edgy enough. But those are the exceptions because kids have accidents and companies eventually realize celery will never be sexy.

So what is the difference?

The graphic designer is a follower of Jesus and understands that the Bible refers to her as a royal priesthood. This means, among other things, that she lives her story before the audience of God, so nothing in her story is hidden from his eyes. God sees all and God cares about all he sees. She reads God into her work, into designing each package for organic apple slices or chicken raised without steroids. She sees God as emotionally invested in her story, wanting her to live it in the most compelling way possible. Have you ever thought of God in those terms? As emotionally invested in the story of your life? He is, and an understanding of calling will help you read God and meaning into seemingly ordinary work.

The third-grade teacher is not a Christ follower. She is still performing an admirable contribution to society by nurturing her third graders in a healthy educational environment. She is not doing her work incorrectly, but she would experience a much richer purpose if her view of work were transformed from seemingly ordinary to sacred. That is what Jesus accomplishes when we understand all believers are a royal priesthood. All work is made sacredly important as a result of the calling Jesus has placed on our lives.

"So, whether you eat or drink, or whatever you do, do all to the glory of God" (1 Corinthians 10:31). It is quite interesting that in this verse Paul referred to the most basic, mundane functions of human existence, i.e., eating and drinking. But not just eating or drinking—"whatever you do" in your life should be done in a way that God is made obvious.

I have the privilege of serving an organization dedicated to teaching students how to think, dream, and lead at the feet of Jesus. Each year thousands of students from hundreds of churches all across the United States allow Student Leadership University to become a part of the story they are telling with their lives. Words cannot describe the sense of fulfillment I feel from watching students awaken to their capacity and potential. As I write this, our organization is twenty years old and has witnessed over 120,000 students come through our programs. But one of the most exciting aspects of my job is to see students go on to become those who truly are contributing toward making society better. In our own way we are trying to equip a generation of contributors. This is my job and it is also my calling.

So whether you are a graphic designer or a third-grade teacher, a butcher, baker, or candlestick maker, God should be made obvious in your work as you contribute to society. The question for some of us is, "How do I design graphics differently because of my faith?" While reading God into daily work will define a standard of excellence, determination, and a right attitude, sometimes God will be most obvious simply in our motivations.

God's call is on our lives through church, family, citizen, and contributor, and we must guard against elevating one element of our calling above another. One job is not more important than the other. And as such, our calling can be summarized in the following way:

- I am called to Christ and thus to be a part of his church.
- I am called to be a part of a family.
- I am called to be a citizen who cares about the glory of God in the public square.
- I am called to be a contributor to the betterment of society.

The challenge will always be reading God into the entire floor plan of our lives. My hope is that by viewing life through our calls to church, family, citizen, and contributor, it becomes very clear how the entirety of all the jobs of our lives can be saturated in God's calling. You were made for this; you were called so that you can live with a consciousness of calling.

CHAPTER EIGHT

A HYPOCRITE'S CONFESSION

S o what do you do?"

That question inevitably comes up multiple times when you spend a million miles at thirty thousand feet breathing recycled air and eating warmed-over meals. I used to have a standard answer like, "Well, I'm a pastor who travels and speaks and writes, and I also run an organization that trains students to be leaders." A simple answer to a simple question, but there is one problem. Everything about that statement is consumed with what *I* do. While it's technically correct, of late I have decided such questions and answers serve to only perpetuate something incredibly burdensome about life. Sure, the original question was structured to ask about my employment, but what's really behind the question is, "Who are you?" In other words, who is this strange being who will sit three inches from me for the next two and a half hours?

Life is not so much about what we can accomplish but about living in what Christ has accomplished. My personal fear is that sometimes I preach and teach about what Christ has accomplished but live as though what matters most is what I can accomplish. It's hypocritical and exhausting. I am now realizing that if I can fully accomplish certain tasks and projects on my own, then the gospel probably isn't at the center of my endeavors. An even tougher thought is knowing God has not called us to do more; he has called us to find rest in him. I love Eugene Peterson's rendering of what Jesus said in Matthew 11:28–30:

> Are you tired? Worn out? Burned out on religion? Come to me. Get away with me and you'll recover your life. I'll show you how to take a real rest. Walk with me and work with me—watch how I do it. Learn the unforced rhythms of grace. I won't lay anything heavy or ill-fitting on you. Keep company with me and you'll learn to live freely and lightly. (MSG)

Take a moment, ponder the above statement, and then ask yourself, "Does this describe the way I am living?" What if we have misunderstood "the race" (Hebrews 12:1) that is our lives? What if the race was not to run faster, harder, and accomplish more, but to struggle, keeping our eyes on Jesus in all things and at all times so that we do not bear more burdens but actually less? Maybe that is why verse 3 reads, "Consider him who endured from sinners such hostility against himself, so that you may not grow weary or faint-hearted." The race is really an interesting metaphor to describe the tension to "lay aside every weight, and sin which clings so closely." And if this makes sense, then the race actually becomes rest when we lay aside all that is unnecessary and sinful to be in a healthy relationship with Jesus. So the goal, and what God is calling us to, is that the race becomes rest . . . and this brings us back to Jesus' words: "Come to me, all of you who are weary and carry heavy burdens, and I will give you rest" (Matthew 11:28).

HIS TEARS ARE BIGGER

In C. S. Lewis's *The Magician's Nephew*, from the Chronicles of Narnia, a little boy and girl named Digory and Polly go on a series of magical adventures involving rings that can transport them to a Wood between the Worlds. Here there are many pools, some leading to other worlds. Thus, the Wood between the Worlds serves as a catalyst, or an in-between place, by which they can return home to England or continue discovering new places. The children decide to explore new worlds and in so doing discover the ancient and desolate land of Charn. It is here that Digory disregards an inscription on a bell that reads:

Make your choice, adventurous Stranger
Strike the bell and bide the danger
Or wonder, till it drives you mad
What would have followed if you had

The choice Digory makes is to ring the bell, and to their surprise this action awakes Queen Jadis, an evil person who has destroyed every living thing in Charn and will later be referred to as the witch. They, including Jadis, eventually end up in Narnia on the very day a huge lion named Aslan roared its creation into existence. All of this happens a thousand years before the next stage of Narnia's history, which can be read about in *The Lion, the Witch, and the Wardrobe*. Bearing shades of original sin, Digory is guilty of bringing Queen Jadis and evil into Narnia on the very day of its conception.

During all of this, Digory is carrying the burden of his mother, who is at home in bed and dying. There seems to be nothing he can do for her until he discovers that the apples from a garden in Narnia contain the power to heal if eaten. A formerly hopeless circumstance now has possibility injected into its narrative. This is the mind-set of young Digory when Aslan confronts him about his guilt for the role he played in bringing Jadis to Narnia. And then Aslan asks him if he's ready to undo the wrong done to Narnia on the very day of its creation. Digory quickly answers yes, but then he wonders if he should ask for Aslan's promise to help his mother as a condition of his participation. But how dare he bargain with the lion? Feeling great distress over his dying hopes and dreams for himself and his mother, Digory blurts out,

> "But please, please—won't you—can't you give me something that will cure my Mother?" Up till then he had been looking at the Lion's great feet and the huge claws on them; now, in his despair, he looked up at its face. What he saw surprised him as much as anything in his whole life. For the tawny face was bent down near his own and (wonder of wonders) great shining tears stood in the Lion's eyes. They were such big, bright tears compared with Digory's own that for a moment he felt as if the Lion must really be sorrier about his Mother than he was himself.[18]

I think a lot of times we are like Digory, carrying around burdens we were never intended to shoulder alone. What a moment it must have been to look up into Aslan's eyes and see that his tears were bigger than Digory's ever could be. That the lion's heart was just as hurt, if not more so, than his own. That in this moment he no longer felt alone and full of despair. Real hope, not the imitation kind of hope that dissipates like foam on the beach, had walked into his life. Can you imagine a little tear streaming down Digory's bright-red cheek and falling to the dirt beneath him? Then a moment later, a bigger tear from above descends, landing on the one tear in the dirt. It was a bigger tear, born from a place of love and concern in the heart of the Creator.

This is what Jesus was telling us when he said, "Take my yoke upon you, and learn from me, for I am gentle and lowly in heart, and you will find rest for your souls. For my yoke is easy, and my burden is light" (Matthew 11:29–30). It is quite liberating to hear Jesus describe the Christian life as "rest." Furthermore, he used imagery from plowing the fields where the ox would be coupled up with a yoke. A yoke is simply a wooden bar that allowed two animals, usually oxen, to be coupled or yoked together, so that they might effectively work together.[19] There is also further meaning when Jesus uses the word *yoke*. Many times the rabbis used it as another reference for school.[20]

Jesus is inviting you to walk with him and learn from him. Jesus wants to shoulder the load so your journey is manageable, effective, and even restful. By sharing the burden, you can finish the race. Alternatively, if you attempt to carry all the burdens yourself, you may very well stumble and fall long before completing the race.

If the burden is heavy, then we are not sharing it with Jesus. If we are not yoked up with Jesus, then we are operating as a functional savior. The person with heavy burdens is oftentimes the exhausted hypocrite whose only response to burdens is to work harder and try more. Jesus is calling us out of our own ability so that we might find synergy with the Savior and in so doing experience rest.

What burdens are you carrying alone? What is weighing you down? A sick loved one? A view of success that depends completely on you? A desire to please? Insecurity of some kind? Whatever it is, we have all been in Digory's shoes at some point or another. We have all carried a burden we were never intended to shoulder alone. So today recognize that God's tears are bigger, and only he can make your burden light.

THE MOST WE CAN ACCOMPLISH IS STILL REFRIGERATOR ART

I love it when my kids make pictures for me. Whether they paint, use crayons, or sketch something, it always warms my heart when I receive the gift of art from one of my children. I love the explanations that accompany the artwork because each picture is really a deep, rich, colorful story. I sit and listen as the art is explained and the story is told. It may sound a bit silly, but I treasure each of those pictures. If you were to come into my home office, where this book is being written, you would not find my walls decorated with diplomas, awards, or any kind of recognitions. Come to think of it, I don't even know where my diplomas are—probably in the attic sandwiched between Christmas decorations and other stuff we should throw away but don't because of sentimental value. In my office you will see a wall littered with artwork from my children over the years. Presently I am looking at a picture my son, Gabe, made when he was six, with the words "Daddy, I love guy time!" There is another that my daughter Charis colored of Tigger from *Winnie the Pooh*. And one my youngest daughter, Mercy, made full of color with the words "I love you more!" You see, every night when I put my kids to bed I always say, "Daddy loves you high as the sky and deep as the ocean." Lately Mercy has been responding, "Yes, but I love you more than that!"

But before any one picture can be added to my gallery, it rests on display in the most prominent place in the house: the refrigerator. This, of course, is a common practice for displaying children's artwork. The fridge is a far cry from a museum, and the art has no monetary value. No, we prominently display our children's "masterpieces" because they made them and we love our kids. We don't affirm the pictures' value to the house but the child's value to the parent.

In the grand scheme of life, I believe the most any one person can ever accomplish—even if given a hundred lifetimes—in the end is nothing more than refrigerator art. I am not suggesting that our refrigerator art does not matter; of course it does. Nor am I suggesting that we should not do our best, set goals, and accomplish projects. I am suggesting that we should create while resting in our Father's love for us.

What I mean by this is that you and I can trust God to create a masterpiece through our life. We are not the heroes of the story that God is telling. God has not rolled the dice hoping that we will get it right so in the end everything will turn out okay. We are not the hope of mankind. We offer hope, rescue, redemption, and purpose through the message of the gospel, but only God can actually accomplish those things in someone.

Our actions should be borne from a place of rest and then carry us on from there. This is what Jesus wants to teach us. He wants us to turn our heads and see him. We are co-laborers with the King, yoked with Jesus by grace and love. This is what we have been called to. Calling is not about *doing more*; rather, it is about *living more* in connection with Jesus. So let us view calling not through the lens of accomplishment, but from the perspective that we can rest in the callings that God has called us to . . . because Jesus has called us to himself and in so doing he has called us to rest.

————

Calling is all about learning the unforced rhythms of grace. We were never intended to be defined by what we do; we are to be defined by who we are. Our lives are supposed to be one big response to the desires of God. Calling is all about pursuing the identity God provides for us as opposed to trying to create our own sense of identity through our family, career, or a role we play. Some may think that much of what I have written in this section is just a matter of semantics. I can hear the devil's advocate in my own head saying, "Yeah, Brent, but by *pursuing* something aren't we really *doing* something?" Maybe, or maybe not.

Could it be that the pursuit and response to God's callings on our life are really about receiving the identity we were always intended to embrace? I think I like this approach better because it forces me to ponder God's sufficiency for my life as opposed to what I can accomplish for myself in an effort to live up to a false picture of the Christian life. When we walk with Jesus in our churches and families, as citizens and contributors to culture, then life's race becomes restful.

THURSDAY

ENGAGEMENT

INTRODUCTION

MARINATING METAPHORS

CHAPTER NINE

SALT: THE FELLOWSHIP OF THE CONCERNED

CHAPTER TEN

LIGHT: THE FELLOWSHIP OF ILLUMINATION

CHAPTER ELEVEN

THE WAYBACK MACHINE

MARINATING METAPHORS

Every year I have the incredible opportunity of journeying through Israel, Jordan, and a couple of Palestinian territories with hundreds of students who are part of the Student Leadership University experience. Nothing that can prepare a seventeen-year-old for experiencing the land where Jesus walked. All of a sudden these young people are given a canvas upon which their imaginations can envision and paint the stories in the Bible. During the trip there are so many rich moments, such as baptizing students in the Jordan River, taking communion outside the garden tomb, and collecting smooth stones from the dry riverbed in the valley where David fought Goliath. But no doubt the most beautiful scene is looking out across the Sea of Galilee from the Mount of Beatitudes where Jesus preached his most famous sermon. The Mount of Beatitudes is located on the northwestern shore of the Sea of Galilee between Capernaum, Jesus' hometown, and Gennesaret.

The landscape, unlike so many other places in the Middle East, is rich with flowers and grassy hills that are so beautiful they almost seem otherworldly. The mount contains flowing hills accompanied with stretches of leveled-off areas, creating a perfect amphitheater setting for Jesus to articulate his message. I love standing on the balcony of a Catholic chapel that was built in the late 1930s by the Franciscan Sisters. Because of the topography, there is always a gentle breeze causing the vines from the bougainvillea plants with their beautiful shades of purple to sway and dance across the chapel grounds. I take great pleasure in looking down toward the sea and observing how the entire landscape seems to exist in a harmonious, well-choreographed dance until at last the music stops at the water's edge, only to make room for another symphony of beauty with the sea itself. It is a setting bursting forth with glorious Technicolor.

It was in this place that Jesus taught citizens of God's kingdom how to function in a world broken by sin. Matthew 5–7 is manifesto-like as Jesus paints a holistic picture of what a pilgrim looks like as he or she journeys home. In short, the Sermon on the Mount is how Jesus wants us to live, and it is a countercultural approach to be sure. These teachings begin in chapter 5 with a series of poetic statements focusing on our relationship with God. Then he turned a very sharp corner, transitioning from our being blessed by God to living out that blessing in culture. To accomplish this Jesus used two simple metaphors: *you are salt* and *you are light*. A life saturated and marinating in blessings that can only come from God is a blessing to the world.

I am not much of a cook. In fact, my few attempts to actually cook a meal for my family have concluded with pizza being delivered. But one thing I love to do is smoke meat. If you are a vegetarian, please do not judge me and I will try not to judge you. (Honestly, I don't think I will ever understand vegetarians. How can you not love a juicy cheeseburger, fries, and a milkshake? But I digress . . . back to smoking meat.)

One of the more important things I have learned about a finished product full of flavor is the process of marinating the meat. To marinate meat is to soak it in seasoning for a period of time so that the flavor saturates the meat and even tenderizes it. If I am going to smoke a brisket or a turkey for the weekend, Thursday is when I marinate the meat. If I marinate it then and smoke the meat on Friday, we can enjoy it all weekend long. So I set aside Thursday to understand how God wants our lives to be saturated with salt and light. These two metaphors paint one picture of a fellowship of people down through the ages living out blessings from on high.

CHAPTER NINE

SALT: THE FELLOWSHIP OF THE CONCERNED

There are those whose life story is stamped with purpose. You can always tell when someone's narrative is marinated daily in a commitment to what matters most. Those types of people are obvious because they are saturated with salt. Their very existence makes the immediate culture in which they live better on so many levels. They understand that to be in Christ is also to be part of his mission for engaging culture. And they live out the words of Jesus when he said, "You are the salt of the earth, but if salt has lost its taste, how shall its saltiness be restored? It is no longer good for anything except to be thrown out and trampled under people's feet" (Matthew 5:13). John Stott articulated this sentiment well when he wrote:

> It is exceedingly strange that any followers of Jesus Christ should ever have needed to ask whether social involvement was their concern, and that controversy should have blown up over the relationship between evangelism and social responsibility. For it is evident that in his public ministry Jesus both "went about . . . teaching . . . and preaching" (Matthew 4:23; 9:35 RSV) and "went about doing good

and healing" (Acts 10:38 RSV). In consequence, evangelism and social concern have been intimately related to one another throughout the history of the Church . . . Christian people have often engaged in both activities quite unselfconsciously, without feeling any need to define what they were doing or why.[1]

And this brings us to the chief aim of our Lord's teaching in this section of the sermon. We engage, to use Stott's term *unselfconsciously*, because it is a natural part of our identity. We do not engage because we decide it is now a good thing to do after we begin our Christian journey, but rather we engage because the goodness of God in Christ Jesus has now saturated our spiritually dead corpses, giving us a purpose that flows outward because of a blessing that has flowed downward from heaven. Again Stott helps inform our understanding of the word *engagement*, meaning "turning our faces toward the world in compassion, getting our hands dirty, sore and worn in its service, and feeling deep within us the stirring of the love of God which cannot be contained."[2] The question then becomes, how do we engage the culture around us?

FELLOWSHIP AND THE SONG OF GOD'S JUSTICE

Engagement begins with the understanding of the phrase "you are." The word *you* is plural and speaks of all Christians throughout time. The word *are* makes these phrases statements of fact. Because of our faith in Jesus, we are now salt. We are part of a fellowship that has existed since Jesus first spoke these words on a hillside to a bunch of Palestinian working-class families so many years ago. Our cultural engagement is rich in heritage; in other words, we are part of something much bigger than one lifetime. "I have decided to follow Jesus" means I have joined in the chorus that is the song of God's justice.[3] What beautiful music sounds when the landscape of history is surveyed and the song of God's justice is being sung.

In his book *How Christianity Changed the World*, Alvin Schmidt surveyed the landscape of how people transformed by Jesus have been transforming the world around them for two thousand years. He concluded, "The lives that Jesus transformed in turn changed and transformed much of the world: its morals, ethics, health care, education, economics, science, law, the fine arts, and government."[4]

Jesus' first metaphor, which is true of all Christ followers, is that we are to be salt. Many different uses for salt can be identified from the Bible and history during this time frame. Just a few examples are:

- Salt was used to symbolize a covenant in 2 Chronicles 13:5 and Leviticus 2:13. It was associated with covenants or sacred agreements because of its durability and incorruption.[5]
- Salt was used as a form of payment for a Roman soldier: "The soldier who was 'not worth his salt' had not earned his 'salary' (a word derived from the Latin word for 'salt')."[6]
- Salt was used as a preservative for meats and fish.
- Salt was a sign of friendship and still is in many Middle Eastern cultures today.

- Rabbis viewed salt as a metaphor for wisdom.[7]
- Salt was sprinkled on newborn babies in Ezekiel 16:4 after the baby had been washed of all fluids to dry and firm the skin.
- Elisha used salt to heal the water of the spring of Jericho in 2 Kings 2:20.

The list could go on and on, but the more we look, the more a correlation of purpose seems to emerge. In virtually every case, salt was used as an agent of protection and preservation. In other words, salt prevented something from being spoiled. If it was diluted in the least, as some would do by adding white sand, then it was rendered useless, purposeless, and pointless. Why? Because salt diluted or made impure cannot protect or preserve. If it is not pure, it cannot fulfill its purpose.

So what does this metaphor mean for us? Because we have placed our faith in Christ Jesus and seen the unseen (Colossians 1:15 says Jesus is the image of the invisible God) and because we have begun to grasp the grandness of God's story (which can only be understood by studying the Bible), then we are an element of preservation and protection for a morally corrupt and spiritually blind world. In other words, we protect and preserve the blind so that they may one day see.

In a day and age before electricity and refrigeration, salt was the only thing that could preserve dead meat. Salt was the one agent that could give something dead and lifeless purpose for another day. We Christians walk among the tombstones in this world, to use the title of a Lawrence Block novel. We live surrounded by people who have eternity placed in their hearts but no hope on the foreseeable horizon. Our mission should be to help the hopeless hold on until hope arrives. We are to sing the song of God's justice and to preserve culture and life, not because a person asks us but because God invites us to engage and to preserve others for the gospel. This is in fact our identity in Christ.

JESUS DID NOT SAY, "YOU ARE SUGARY SWEET"

Jesus did not say we are honey or sugary sweet. By this I mean Jesus did not call us to engage people with false hope. This is the type of person who erases all responsibility, accountability, and consequences from life. This person shares a message through actions or words that gives false security based on unfounded optimism. To communicate that "everything is okay and you will be okay" is to abuse grace and make it cheap. The message of the gospel is not "everything is okay, so let's just comfort each other." Rather, the message of the gospel is, "Everything was okay before we destroyed it! But then Jesus came to offer us hope, and in him everything can be okay once again."

Those who just want to be sugary sweet all the time will never confront sin and will always conform to the world. Part of being salt is that we stand on the front lines against racism, poverty, disease, natural disaster, and a plethora of other inequities. Why? Because that is who we are. To be salt is to say, "Injustice cannot be tolerated on my watch." It is to stand in the arena of culture—for example, against abortion or gay marriage when everyone is cheering death upon us—and shout, "In the name of Jesus, this must stop!" Our job is not to sing a song while the *Titanic* is sinking so everyone is happy while they are dying. May it never be! Our job, because of our identity, is to get everyone on a life raft until a ship appears on the horizon to offer a permanent fix.

JESUS DID NOT SAY, "YOU ARE SPICY HOT"

While the sugary sweet person never confronts, the spicy hot person is always confronting. This is the type of person who lives perched on a soapbox telling others what they should do and not do with their lives. The problem with that kind of militant spirit is, it points out more of one's personality than the person and love of Jesus. Those who are confrontational and divisive leave others feeling like hope will never show up, so people feel defeated.

I have found divisive people think they know the problem well but do not know the people who are involved in the problem. As I heard author and activist Bob Goff say once, "People create problems, but people are not problems." Those who are always contentious watch riots and make conclusions without ever getting to know one person involved in the riot. They make sweeping generalizations about those in the LBGT community but have never shared a meal with someone who embraces that lifestyle.

The bottom line is that we can never help someone into the life raft if we don't get close enough to give him or her directions to it. It is impossible to be a preserving force for good when we are divorced from relationships. Salt only preserves when it is applied, that is, when it interacts with that which it is meant to preserve. And salt only works when it is pure and undiluted. A failure to remain pure and a failure to interact make the entire purpose of salt null and void. Jesus said that at that point we are "no longer good for anything except to be thrown out and trampled under people's feet." Failing to engage in the world as devoted followers of Jesus renders our lives pointless.

The message from this metaphor is simple: stay engaged, realizing success may simply mean helping someone hold on for one more day. Promise someone that hope exists, that the present situation is not as good as it gets, and wait with him or her in the life raft until somewhere out on the horizon a steam liner appears.

CHAPTER TEN

LIGHT: THE FELLOWSHIP OF ILLUMINATION

Jesus is the light of the world. He does not have an on or off switch and cannot be compared to any light controlled by human hands. "He is light" means that light is part of his identity and cannot be understood separate from the name of Jesus. He has never been given light, but rather he has always been light and he will always be light. His light is eternal and unlimited. He requires no fuel, no electricity, and no battery. The light of the world needs no energy source. Why? Because God will never become less than God. He is, in some supernatural way beyond human understanding, self-sufficient. He is so powerful that he can illuminate the darkest corners and the farthest reaches of this world and never run out of light.

Louie Giglio, pastor of Passion City Church in Atlanta, stated it this way in a sermon: "If Jesus is the light of the world then our salvation is an event of light."[8] In our salvation we move from spiritual darkness to spiritual light. Imagine being born blind and spending a lifetime in darkness. Then all of a sudden a miracle drug or treatment is offered to you and all you have to do is accept it. Living in darkness and always longing for something more, such an offer seems irresistible and almost too good to be true.

Now imagine that the treatment works! For the first time in your entire life you see grass and flowers, people holding hands and little kids running up to their parents in the park, clouds and the seemingly endless beauty of a blue sky; for the first time you see creation.

In essence, what has taken place is the entirety of your existence has now awakened to a different life of possibility and purpose. Jesus is the light of the world that chases out the darkness in our lives so that we can live illuminated. Jesus applied illumination, light, to how we should then engage the world: "You are the light of the world. A city set on a hill cannot be hidden. Nor do people light a lamp and put it under a basket, but on a stand, and it gives light to all in the house. In the same way, let your light shine before others, so that they may see your good works and give glory to your Father who is in heaven" (Matthew 5:14–16).

EXTERIOR LIGHTING

Jesus spoke of light in two different ways, as exterior and interior, both with the same function. First, he spoke of light as a city on a hill. The purpose of the light metaphor is that our lives are to illuminate others toward the goodness of God in Christ Jesus. While salt is for preserving against corruption, light is for chasing away darkness and shining a light on truth. Just as our personal salvation was an event of light, so we are to shine that light for all to see in whatever city we live in. We are called to light up the dark in the world according to Jesus' words.

When I first considered these words, my thought was, *Yeah, but isn't Jesus the light of the world?* After all, Jesus said in John 9:5, "As long as I am in the world, I am the light of the world." Or consider John 8:12 when he said, "I am the light of the world. Whoever follows me will not walk in darkness, but will have the light of life." There exists the great purpose of this statement, and all of the Sermon on the Mount for that matter. Jesus was saying that we are to be like him in illuminating the world to another possibility and purpose for this thing called life. The light that we shine is not our own but is the light of Jesus radiating through us. Scottish theologian William Barclay stated it this way: "The radiance which shines from the Christian comes from the presence of Christ within the Christian's heart."[9]

There can be no mistaking the audacity and reach of Jesus' metaphor when he compared the Christian to a city in the world. Our influence and engagement should never be limited and should always be brave and courageous. One man or woman carrying the light of Jesus can light up the dark in an entire city, nation, or world. I like the way Bob Goff, in his bestseller *Love Does*, said it:

> Being engaged is a way of doing life, a way of living and loving. It's about going to extremes and expressing the bright hope that life offers us, a hope that makes us brave and expels darkness with light. That's what I want my life to be all about—full of abandon, whimsy, and love. I want to be engaged to life and with life.[10]

INTERIOR LIGHTING

We further see how the gospel is to be broadcasted with the light illuminating an entire household. First, a little context is needed to more accurately understand Jesus' words. Most homes would have a small wicker oil lamp that would illuminate a house; many times a home would simply be one room. To maximize the illumination, they would put the lamp in the middle of the house so the light could reach the farthest corners. Jesus painted a picture of how ludicrous it would be to take a basket, which was a measuring bowl for grain and would have existed in the home of every listener that day, and cover up the lamp. To do so would probably extinguish the light, rendering the lamp useless!

Jesus is calling us not only to illuminate the far reaches of the world but the ones closest to us on a daily basis. Light that seeks to chase out the darkness in a third-world country but tolerates darkness next door is not really light . . . it is just an act. It would be quite hypocritical to be a witness in other parts of the world but not at home or in our closest relationships, because the very nature of light is illumination, wherever that light may exist. This is our Savior's desired point with both comparisons.[11] He longs for us to live consistent with who he is and reflect his light *everywhere* because of our identities in him.

We belong to a fellowship of renegade Christ followers who have been lighting up the dark world one house at a time for two thousand–plus years. We carry with us the light of Jesus and the legacy of witnesses who have gone before us. We carry on because grace leaves us with no other option and because obscurity is for those who don't really understand the gospel. The community of God is a place where his light shines. Since the very nature of light is to illuminate, it cannot help but engage the darkness. And this, I write cautiously, brings us to an unfortunate reality: if you are not shining any light interiorly or exteriorly, then there is no Jesus in your life.

THE CONJUNCTION THAT MAKES ENGAGEMENT FUNCTION

In closing this chapter I want to draw our attention to a little, albeit implied, conjunction with a giant function. The importance of the word *and* cannot be underestimated. I know what you're thinking: *The word doesn't appear in the text.* Never fear, I have not completely lost my mind. That we are to be salt *and* light is very much implied in the text in that Jesus was using two metaphors to paint a picture of one Christian engaged in culture. Some of us may feel very comfortable meeting felt needs, walking in marches against injustice, or sponsoring an impoverished child through a relief organization. These are amazing things, to be sure! Others may feel strongly toward evangelism and telling people about Jesus through different strategies and methods. This is equally important. Efforts to preserve culture independent from sharing Jesus, and sharing Jesus independent of protecting culture from moral corruption, are both incomplete pictures.

Jesus very clearly made two statements of fact concerning all Christians. In other words, *and* is implied. Being salt is all about preserving culture, so we are to be on the front lines against injustice. That means the transgender student being bullied on a high school campus should have the protection of some Jesus followers. It means when racism rears its ugly head, people who love Jesus should seek to understand the problem and stand with the victims of this evil. It also means that when a natural disaster such as an earthquake or a tsunami occurs, Christians should be the first to shoulder the burden of loss and pain. We do this because it is all evidence of a broken world that we helped corrupt. We do this because when Jesus chased out the darkness in our lives, we became compassionately aware of darkness throughout our world.

But preserving and protecting are not enough. Jesus bids us to live in such a way that we illuminate others to his love. We stand up for those being bullied, care for those being victimized, and bring relief to those who have lost homes and even family members, all in the name of Jesus. We are salt *and* light. If we are just salt, then we'll become the heroes of our own stories, the functional savior to the poor and plighted. If we are just light, we become those who stand on a mountaintop and shout down at sinners below the good news of Jesus. But good news is not heard through an echo; rather, it is seen and heard through the personal interaction that can only come from engagement. The importance of *and* is this: that through our engagement, people will look to the God of heaven because they have experienced a little bit of heaven by meeting us. Who would have ever thought that there was so much power in such a little word? The importance of the *and* is that it is the conjunction that makes engagement function.

THE WAYBACK MACHINE

B elow is a list of names from a time long ago. A casual scan of each name might lead you to think they were important in their respective fields and era. Though such a verdict would be right, if they had lived and led independent of each other, or even if one or two had occasionally worked together on a project here and there, their names would likely have been lost to dusty history books. But theirs is a different story. Theirs is a story of a community of men and women who would not relent until they had transformed the world around them. I like to consider this list as history's greatest case study in salt and light.

- Hannah More (1745–1835): poet, playwright, and educational reformer
- Granville Sharp (1735–1813): biblical scholar and abolitionist pioneer
- Henry Thornton (1760–1815): William Wilberforce's second cousin and cofounder of the Clapham Sect; a merchant banker and MP for Southwark
- Zachary Macaulay (1768–1838): estate manager of a

sugar plantation in Jamaica; colonial governor of the Sierra Leone colony for emancipated slaves

- James Stephen (1758–1832): gifted lawyer who specialized in the laws governing Great Britain's foreign trade; author who focused on the slave trade and the West Indies
- Edward James Eliot (1758–97): parliamentarian
- Thomas Gisbourne (1758–1846): author and Anglican priest
- Lord Teignmouth, formerly John Shore (1751–1834): spent five years as governor; general of India; first president of the British and Foreign Bible Society
- Charles Grant (1746–1823): politician who focused on the spread of Christianity in India; chairman of British East India Company
- Thomas Babington (1758–1837): philanthropist and politician
- Thomas Fowell Buxton (1786–1845): politician; brewer; following William Wilberforce's retirement he took up the cause in parliament; helped found the Anti-Slavery Society; Elizabeth Fry's brother-in-law
- Dr. Isaac Milner (1750–1820): mathematician; president of Queen's College, Cambridge; instrumental in William Wilberforce's religious conversion
- Charles Simeon (1759–1836): clergyman; considered a leader among evangelical clergymen and cofounder of Church Missionary Society

With William Wilberforce's leadership and campaign to abolish slavery as the epicenter, these names make up a group of people who affected more change than maybe any other group of their size in history. They were commonly called the "Clapham Sect" or "Clapham Group," and members of the community were referred to as "Claphamites" and eventually earned the nickname of "Saints." The Clapham Sect was a group of people who decided together to wrap their arms around the world in the name of Jesus. They decided to squeeze out injustice by being salt and light.

In 1792, Wilberforce settled at Clapham, where he became, along with Henry Thornton, the founding member of the Clapham Sect.[12] Clapham was a pastoral village in Surrey located just outside of London. It was here that this company of reformers would converse, strategize, and pray for reform. John Venn was brought in by Henry Thornton to be the pastor of Clapham's parish church. He taught about a more openly evangelical gospel than had been previously preached,[13] in other words, one that encouraged engagement.

Politician and historian William Hague described the group as being

> [w]holly relaxed in each other's company . . . The intimacy they developed was remarkable, it being their custom "to consider every member of that community as forming part of a large united family, who should behave to each other with the same simplicity and absence of formality, which, in the usual way, characterizes intercourse only among the nearest relatives."[14]

The central cause that dominated Claphamite thinking was the abolition of the slave trade; however, the efforts made by the group the twelve years following 1792 "ultimately led to one of the greatest varieties and volumes of charitable activity ever launched by any group of people in any age."[15, 16] John Piper credited, in part, the Clapham Sect with providing Wilberforce the fuel to stay engaged in the face of constant opposition. He wrote, "The achievement of Wilberforce's vision is largely attributable to the value he and his colleagues placed on harnessing their diverse skills while submitting their egos for the greater public good."[17]

Historian John Pollock summarized concerning the Clapham Sect, "Wilberforce is proof that a man can change his times, though he cannot do it alone."[18] One of the members of the sect whom Wilberforce frequently corresponded with was Hannah More. An example of his admiration for Mrs. More can be seen in a letter he wrote to her during a contentious debate over abolition dated November 9, 1796:

> How I respect your exertions, I would say to any one rather than you; but to your feeling it will afford a cordial, to be assured that a friend looks through the bustling crowd with which he is hemmed in, and fixes his eye on you with complacency and approbation—God knows that I wish to imitate your example, and to learn from you to seize the short intervals of tolerable ease and possible action, for acting for the suppression of vice and alleviation of misery.[19]

The Claphamite strategy sacredly and simply provides us an incredible example of the synergetic power that exists when a group of people is committed to being salt and light. They were bound together by a common faith and belief that the gospel, when properly understood, demands engagement. They were poets and playwrights, bankers and brewers, preachers and politicians, and they all met at the foot of the cross. Historically, people with wealth and influence have been involved with charities in the margins of life, but the Clapham Sect believed engagement was to be at the center of their stories. We can easily conclude that when Jesus is at the center of our friendships and communities, then justice is valued throughout the world.

The group made the decision to all live in the same village, which would afford them the ability to have an ongoing conversation centered on each other's causes. They leveraged influence and resources for each other, worshipped together, laughed and cried together, and quite simply did life together.

They were a group of people who loved Jesus, had influence, believed the gospel demanded justice, and collaborated toward that goal. In an age long before social media and instant messaging, the Internet and e-mail, or even Edison's inventions, it is amazing that this group had such an impact. In an attempt to demonstrate the far-reaching and lasting impact of one group of people who lived in community for a handful of years, I turn again to the research of Hague. Here I summarize from the accomplishments of the Clapham Sect in the twelve years following 1792:

- Promoted charity schools in Ireland
- Started a shelter that provided help to deaf and mentally handicapped children for parents who couldn't afford proper care
- Created avenues for relief for the poor in London
- Launched education initiatives in Africa

- Created a refuge for orphan girls
- Founded the following:
  - The Society for Religious Instruction to the Negroes in the West Indies
  - The London Missionary Society
  - The Society for Bettering the Condition and Increasing the Comforts of the Poor
  - The Church Missionary Society
  - The Religious Tract Society
  - The Society for Promoting the Religious Instruction of Youth
  - The Society for the Relief of the Industrious Poor
  - The British National Endeavor for the Orphans of Soldiers and Sailors
  - The Naval Society for the Support of the Orphans and Children of British Sailors and Marines
  - The Institution for the Protection of Young Girls
  - The Society of the Suppression of Vice
  - The Sunday School Union
  - The Society for Superseding the Necessity for Climbing-Boys in Cleansing Chimneys
  - The British and Foreign Bible Society
  - The Friendly Female Society, for the Relief of Poor, Infirm, Aged Widows, and Single Women of Good Character, Who Have Seen Better Days

Out of a deep concern for health care needs, just in London they founded a cancer hospital, a fever hospital, two eye clinics, and a multiplicity of medical societies and walk-in medical clinics.[20] And it must be noted that other than the abolition of the slave trade, sending missionaries to India was of utmost concern among the Clapham Sect.

While all of this seems a bit overwhelming and impressive, it was all part of Wilberforce's plan to abolish the slave trade. Scarcely more than a year after his spiritual transformation, which he referred to as "the great change," on Sunday, October 28, 1787, he found his life's work. On a blank page of his diary he wrote, "God Almighty has set before me *two great objects*, the suppression of the slave trade and the reformation of manners."[21] Though God had set two great objects before Wilberforce, both were part of one vision to bring about change.

Wilberforce's strategy to abolish the slave trade would include a revival of morality, thus creating a culture within which abolition of the trade would be a popular and logical action. In other words, the second great object, the reformation of manners, would facilitate a context or culture that would be more open to the first great object, the demise of the slave trade. The Clapham Sect made morality in England popular again, so that the whole of culture would be open to the idea of abolition and eventual emancipation. They made history for bringing about the greatest social change the world has ever seen by simply doing life together at the feet of Jesus.

While Las Vegas may be the modern-day city that never sleeps, a sleepy little village outside of London named Clapham, which no one had ever heard of, became the city that never stopped serving. Today we choose where we want to live for a variety of reasons, including school districts, proximity to our jobs, size of homes and its distance to nice restaurants and shopping. None of these are necessarily bad reasons. But what if we were wholly devoted to changing our world to the point that it determined where we lived, whom we were intimately connected with, and how we spent our leisure time? What if we decided to be part of a community galvanized by the gospel and a commitment to engagement? What if ours was a story that we wouldn't relent until we had transformed our culture in such a way that history would look back and conclude, "They were a people that met at the cross, they were a people that changed their times."

Salt and light. A sacredly simplistic strategy that when employed leads to others seeing our good works and glorifying our Father in heaven.

RELATIONSHIPS

INTRODUCTION

ROCKET SHIPS AND CANDY

CHAPTER TWELVE

DOCTORS AND PATIENTS

CHAPTER THIRTEEN

COLLABORATION: WE > ME

ROCKET SHIPS AND CANDY

I like to tell stories while our family is finishing dinner. Sometimes my kids will shout out things like, "Tell a story that involves a spaceship!" or "Tell us one that has lots of candy and treats!" And because they are children and their imaginations have not yet been corrupted by reality, they see no reason why spaceships and candy cannot coexist in the same story. Such was a recent request.

One day three little children were playing in the backyard and having an enormous amount of fun. In fact, the sun was starting to set and the lightning bugs were lighting up the dark so the children played on, laughing the evening away without a care in the world. Soon stars began to appear in the night's sky and the two girls and little boy lay flat on the grass staring up at them. With their heavy breathing finally slowing down, hair damp from perspiration, and blue jeans streaked with grass stains, their imaginations focused vertically. A conversation ensued about space travel to other worlds and what it would be like to soar through the heavens.

One of the little girls then stated in a rather confident

voice, "I'm going to be there first to travel among the stars and see other planets!"

Surprisingly, no one voiced an objection but rather said, "Can we come?" and "You wouldn't go on such a journey without me!" That evening three little kids devised a plan to build a rocket ship and spend an upcoming summer vacation traveling among the stars.

The little girl who had spoken with such confidence also had a knack for putting things together. Therefore, this little engineer in the making sketched out a list of supplies necessary to build the rocket ship. The boy and the other little girl served as manual labor, always on an errand to get another part necessary for the ship. The children were careful to carry on the construction in an open patch in the woods that their mother could not see from the back porch window. At first the project seemed slow and impossible, but something amazing happens when imagination and determination collide.

Month by month went by with progress coming slowly but surely. Early signs of fall turned into the chill of winter. Then Christmas decorations came down and spring followed shortly thereafter. By the end of March it had become obvious that the improbable (some would say *impossible*) was beginning to take shape. The rocket ship was completed a couple of weeks before school let out for summer break. During this time, the three children collected necessary supplies like food, water, and clothes for their journey.

The three gathered in the opening in the woods the morning after school had been dismissed. Each took his or her seat inside the ship that had taken nine months to construct. The "little engineer that could" pushed buttons and verbalized a countdown. With each passing number, each child's heart rate soared . . . 5 . . . 4 . . . The rocket shook . . . 3 . . . 2 . . . 1 . . .

BLAST OFF!

The children were above the tree line in no time at all, and soon the earth below shrunk smaller and smaller while the horizon in front of them grew wider and wider.

The children could hardly believe it! They were flying through space and could now go wherever they wanted! The little engineer set her sights on a pink planet not too far away. When the rocket ship landed on the pink planet, it almost felt as if they were setting down on a pillow or a pile of feathers. The little boy was the first to step foot outside the rocket ship. He proceeded with grown-up-like caution and carefully stepped onto the planet. When he placed his foot on the surface of the pink planet, he sank up to his knees in something fluffy. He turned and nodded to the two girls as if to say, "Come on down and check this out."

Once the two girls were standing on the planet, all three looked at each other, trying to figure out exactly what this strange fluffy material was that they were standing in.

A few moments later the youngest child blurted out, "It's cotton candy!" The boy and the other girl turned around to see her with a full hand of the pink cotton candy and evidence around the corners of her mouth that she had sampled it.

Having explored the planet and consumed some of its sugary goodness, they took off to discover another planet. They found a planet made completely out of Twizzlers and one made of nothing but milk chocolate complete with chocolate lakes and rivers. With each stop they enjoyed what the planet had to offer before blasting off to discover another. It would turn out to be the greatest summer of their childhood.

In the years that followed their return home, their imagination turned to other, less fantastic things, and soon the summer spent in the rocket ship was a distant memory. Somewhere between being teenagers and becoming adults they were tempted to believe they had made the whole thing up and never really left the open patch in the woods. But each and every time such a thought entered their minds, they closed their eyes and remembered the planets and all the sweet treats they had enjoyed. And for a moment they believed in the impossible again.

I believe we are children staring off into the heavens longing to discover something new. We are pilgrims journeying home to the celestial city, strangers and foreigners searching for where we belong. Just as the children imagined, built, and explored together, so we were created to journey with others. Certainly each individual must make his or her own decision to follow Jesus, but once that faith decision is made, we do not follow him in a vacuum. We are not mavericks following the Master but rather sons and daughters, a community of people who are part of The Way. Ours is a communal faith full of imagination, collaboration, adventure, and discovery. Our relationships are of utmost importance, for the type of relationships we build will determine our capacity to imagine, collaborate, and discover. Through the right relationships we can become better versions of ourselves and help others become better versions of themselves as well. That is what redemption is all about—being brought out of the old and into the new.

On what we Christians refer to as Good Friday, God made a way for us to have a relationship with him through his Son, Jesus. Therefore, it is on this day that we discuss two kinds of relationships. The first is friendship and the second is collaborative relationships. God transforms sinners into saints and enemies into friends, so any type of healthy relationship, whether it be a friendship or a collaborative effort for a cause, is ultimately a reflection of what God made possible on a Friday so long ago.

CHAPTER TWELVE

DOCTORS AND PATIENTS

Between 1942 and 1945, psychiatrist Viktor Frankl labored in four different concentration camps, including Auschwitz, while his parents, brother, and pregnant wife perished. In *Man's Search for Meaning*, he shared his experiences and stories of many of his patients. There may not be another account written that paints a more vivid picture of the Nazi network of concentration and extermination camps. Toward the end of Frankl's imprisonment, he was given the opportunity to escape with a friend. He had agreed to leave the death camp, as anyone in his or her right mind would do. After all, he had already survived a stretch of time at Auschwitz, and there is only so much a person can endure before giving in to death. As the designated time to escape drew near, Frankl made one last round to visit his patients, sick with all kinds of aliments. Upon sitting with a fellow countryman who was nearing death and trying to hide his intentions of escape, the man said to Frankl in a weak and broken voice, "You, too, are getting out?" He denied the question, which felt like an accusation, but could not shake an unpleasant feeling of leaving his sick comrades behind. The following excerpt explains in Frankl's own words what happened next:

Suddenly I decided to take fate into my own hands for once. I ran out of the hut and told my friend that I could not go with him. As soon as I had told him with finality that I had made up my mind to stay with my patients, the unhappy feeling left me. I did not know what the following days would bring, but I had gained an inward peace that I had never experienced before. I returned to the hut, sat down on the boards at my countryman's feet and tried to comfort him; then I chatted with others, trying to quiet them in their delirium.[1]

The idea of leaving a sick and dying comrade behind combined with the stinging words "You, too, are getting out?" seemed to have caused him to discover something greater than escape . . . peace. In the midst of the most hellish situation imaginable, there existed a relationship bound together by a common hope.

UNDERSTANDING FRIENDSHIP

In the end, friendship has as its binding agent that which existed between Dr. Frankl and his countryman patient so many years ago: *hope.* Hope for the patient and hope for the doctor. Hope exists within the experiment of friendship. When we discuss friendship and one's community relationships, we must see ourselves in two very distinct lights: as both doctors and patients. As an inner circle of people following Jesus and walking beside one another, we must recognize the need to care for everyone's souls (the role of doctor) while also allowing our souls to be cared for (the role of patient). Where friendship exists, hope exists. Why? Because Jesus illuminates and informs our thinking concerning hope, in that he makes sinners into friends with God.

I do not know if it is arrogance or naiveté that keeps people from being transparently honest with others about their struggles. As we discovered earlier, God did not create us to live life on our own; rather, he created us as relational beings. I realize that many of us reading this would dismiss such a statement because we prefer to be alone. Here is a shout-out to all my introverts: I am one of you! Though our personalities may tend to be more antisocial, it does not give us an excuse to retreat from having the right kind of relationships in our lives. The ability to walk with others as we walk with Christ is a crucial part of our spiritual formation.

So what are the characteristics of a good friend, a friend who will keep us accountable to the best version of ourselves? A friend who will be a doctor to our soul and allow him or herself to be a patient in need of care? Though the word *accountability* never appears in Scripture, the concept is oftentimes discussed within the context of friendship. Thus, we will define it as follows: "Accountability happens among an inner-circle of friends who care for each other's souls as if they were their own, for the purpose of helping one another be rooted and built up in Jesus and established in the faith."

As with every group of people, a certain culture exists. Within the community in which you live, and particularly among the inner circle of friends you do life with, there is cultural DNA, if you will. For real, healthy, life-giving relationships to exist, we must be willing to fulfill the role of both doctor and patient in administering and receiving the following qualities.

Love

One of the more well-known and compelling stories of friendship in the Bible is that of Jonathan and David. David's friendship with Jonathan, Saul's oldest son, began when David killed Goliath and endured throughout Saul's persecution of David. What we know of their friendship is that Jonathan loved David as if he were his own soul, as evidence from Scripture, which says that "the soul of Jonathan was knit to the soul of David, and Jonathan loved him as his own soul . . . Then Jonathan made a covenant with David, because he loved him as his own soul" (1 Samuel 18:1, 3).

The bond was made official in a ceremony in which Jonathan gave his robe and even his armor to David. Do you catch what is happening here? Jonathan was the prince, heir to the throne, while David was nothing more than a shepherd boy at that point. In that culture, to receive anything that had been *worn* by royalty—or a king's eldest son and heir—was considered the *highest* honor that could be conferred on a subject.[2] Jonathan was expressing that he loved David more than military strength, political power, and even his own life.

If you are a guy and you are reading this, you may be a little uncomfortable with where the application of this text might lead. I know I find it very difficult to tell another guy that I love and care for him. If you have not figured it out, I am not the type of friend who will end every phone call with, "Love you, man." I have friends like that, and I am not saying they are wrong. In fact, sometimes I say it back just so it's not awkward . . . yet saying it still feels a bit strange. There are a select few men in my inner circle, though, to whom I verbalize *philia*, a Greek term for brotherly or friendship-type love. Why? Because, hopefully, I value their life more than I value my own. C. S. Lewis said it this way:

> Friendship is something that raised us almost above humanity. This love, free from instinct, free from all duties but those which love has freely assumed, almost wholly free from jealousy, and free without qualification from the need to be needed, is eminently spiritual. It is the sort of love one can imagine between angels.[3]

Oneness

The type of oneness I'm talking about here is different from the kind found in marriage.

> Two are better than one, because they have a good reward for their toil. For if they fall, one will lift up his fellow. But woe to him who is alone when he falls and has not another to lift him up! Again, if two lie together, they keep warm, but how can one keep warm alone? And though a man might prevail against one who is alone, two will withstand him—a threefold cord is not quickly broken. (Ecclesiastes 4:9–12)

The two lying next to each other refers to those who travel together across deserts and would need to lie next to each other to stay warm during the cold nights. But it is verse 12 that demonstrates oneness in friendship by using the picture of three strands or individuals who have been woven together to create one cord or friendship for the purposes of being able to stand against evil.

The picture painted in these verses is simple: If one falls, the other picks him up (v. 10); if one is cold, then together they can stay warm (v. 11); if one is attacked, the other will have his back (v. 12); two is better than one, and three is better than two (v. 12) because together they form *one* friendship. Friendship should revolve around an "if you go, we go" type attitude. Are you the type of person who refuses to let your friends fall, feel cold, or be beaten down by all the demands of life? I am constantly amazed at the amount of people who attend church or stand in a crowded room and yet feel completely alone. God wants us to be a part of a community of people following Jesus. It never pleases God when there is a tribe of one. So take a moment and think, *What friends have my back, and vice versa, no matter the situation?*

Loyalty

It is better to have one true friend than many casual acquaintances. It is better to have a friend you know in real life than ten thousand who follow you through social media: "A man of many companions may come to ruin, but there is a friend who sticks closer than a brother" (Proverbs 18:24). This verse also indicates that true friendship may be thicker than blood. Matthew Henry stated it this way:

> In our troubles we expect comfort and relief from our relations, but sometimes *there is a friend,* that is nothing akin to us, the bonds of whose esteem and love prove stronger

than those of nature, and, when it comes to the trial, will do more for us than a brother will. Christ is a friend to all believers, that *sticks closer than a brother*; to him therefore let them show themselves friendly.[4]

There is comfort in knowing someone is loyal and trustworthy. It is a trait that, potentially above all others, inspires and motivates. The story is told of two young men in the First World War who had been friends their entire life. They had played together, gone to school together, engaged in the same athletic programs, and finally had enlisted in the army together. Fate determined they would eventually be in the same area of battle.

After a particularly bitter day of fighting, one of the men was missing somewhere out in what is known as "No-Man's Land." The other man, safe and unhurt, went to the commanding officer and requested permission to go out and look for his friend. He was told it was of no use, for no one was alive out there after so many hours of withering gunfire and explosions. After great insistence, though, he was finally given permission to go. Sometime later he came back carrying the limp, lifeless body of his friend over his shoulders. The commander said, "Didn't I tell you it was no use to go?" to which the boy replied with radiance in his eyes, "But it was not; I got there in time to hear him whisper, 'I knew you'd come.'"[5]

Counsel

When your friends think of you, there is always a first thought or a lasting impression usually attached to a pattern of behavior. That impression could either be positive or negative, depending upon the memories associated with you. The first thought then creates an expectation of any encounter. What do your friends expect when they see you coming? The writer of Proverbs used an interesting analogy when describing what can be expected from a true friend: "Oil and perfume make the heart glad, and the sweetness of a friend comes from his earnest counsel" (Proverbs 27:9). This speaks to how the sense of smell can invoke a certain emotion. Maybe it arises because oil and perfume were reserved for honored guests or possibly because the smell was so pleasant that it caused one to feel a certain way. Either way, the result is the same: a glad heart. *The Message* words it well: "Just as lotions and fragrance give sensual delight, a sweet friendship refreshes the soul."

Does the counsel you give, the words you speak to your friends, refresh their souls? Does an encounter with you cause them to experience the same emotion that accompanies the smell of perfume and oil, a heart that is glad? We must be exhaustively intentional with the words we use when advising our friends. This can only be accomplished when our words are filtered through the truth of God's Word. Wise counsel is words that have weight because they are loaded down with God's truth.

Kindness

The story of Job is among the oldest complete pieces of ancient literature in existence. It is beautiful poetry expressing the story of one man, and yet it has a universal appeal because the narrative wrestles with the subject of human suffering. In fact, the theme of the book could be stated in the question, "Why do godly people suffer?" Early on in the book, Job endures a hurricane of suffering in which he loses almost everything he loves. His job as a farmer and rancher is destroyed when all his livestock die (1:13–17);

then all but four of his servants are killed, and all ten of his children die in a freak windstorm (1:18–19). To add insult to injury, he gets a horrible skin disease (2:7). In worldly terms, Job loses everything and is not even welcome in the nearby city. Everyone left alive in his life turns his or her back on him. His wife tells him to "curse God and die!" (2:9). His friends focus most of their efforts on telling Job that his suffering must be his own fault.

In the midst of a conversation with his "friends," and in response to their theologically inaccurate commentary on his circumstances, Job offers a stinging indictment concerning their treatment of him: "He who withholds kindness from a friend forsakes the fear of the Almighty" (Job 6:14). He describes their kindness toward him as overflowing when everything was going well, but empty when things were not. In essence, they are fair-weather friends, who can be defined as people "who [are] dependable in good times but [are] not in times of trouble."[6] He goes on to describe them as a dry riverbed that once flowed with water but dried up in the heat of the summer. Their loyalty and kindness have dried up, and they have treated him deceitfully.

Here we are shown that kindness is essential to friendship, which in Job's case was not demonstrated. The concept of kindness is woven into the fabric of loyalty. In fact, kindness is the attitude demonstrated within loyalty. Think of loyalty as the outer bone while kindness and love are the marrow that runs deep inside it. James took a similar perspective on kindness when he wrote, "For if you refuse to act kindly, you can hardly expect to be treated kindly. Kind mercy wins over harsh judgment every time" (James 2:13 MSG).

Honesty

In the Scripture we read, "Faithful are the wounds of a friend" (Proverbs 27:6). The word *friend* here could also be translated as "one who loves," and the wounds he inflicts are a result of rebuke and correction. True friendship, and therefore accountability, must love in such a courageous manner that one is willing to correct a friend for the purpose of keeping his or her eyes fixed on Jesus, even if it causes pain.

We do not edify by our silence when a friend needs to be rebuked or corrected. The word *rebuke* carries with it a harsh connotation at times, but when this word is understood, it could be the most loving action demonstrated. To rebuke someone simply means to show people the error of their ways by calling them back to a godly approach so they understand and embrace God's way as what's best. This type of honesty is not easy, but it is essential. Remember that to be a true friend means that we function as both doctors and patients. If a doctor's patient has a disease for which there is a cure, but the doctor does nothing about it, he or she is at best a deceitful liar and at worst the devil himself. To observe sin in a friend's life and do nothing about it, I would argue, is the equivalent of a doctor withholding treatment. A real friend is willing to have those tough and honest conversations.

Sacrifice

Jesus commands us to love one another in a sacrificial manner. In fact, one of the ways we know we are abiding in his love is when we are willing to put our lives on the line for our friends: "Greater love has no one than this, than to lay down one's life for his friends"

(John 15:13 NKJV). I find it quite interesting that when Jesus spoke these words, he was soon to lay down his life for each and every one of his friends, not to mention the entire world. But remember, friendship is a two-way street. Would the disciples in turn lay down their lives for Jesus if the opportunity arrived? According to tradition, all of the disciples died a martyr's death:

- Matthew was slain with a sword at a distant city of Ethiopia.
- Mark expired at Alexandria after being cruelly dragged through the streets of that city.
- Luke was hanged upon an olive tree in Greece.
- John was put in a cauldron of boiling oil but escaped death in a miraculous manner and was banished to Patmos.
- Peter was crucified in Rome with his head downward.
- James, the Greater, was beheaded in Jerusalem.
- James, the Less, was thrown from a lofty pinnacle of the temple and then beaten to death with a fuller's club.
- Bartholomew was flayed alive.
- Andrew was bound to a cross, from which he preached to his persecutors until he died.
- Thomas was run through with a lance in Coromandel in the East Indies.
- Jude was shot to death with arrows.
- Matthias was first stoned and then beheaded.
- Barnabas of the Gentiles was stoned to death in Salonica.
- Paul, after various tortures and persecutions, was beheaded in Rome by Emperor Nero.[7]

While there are larger amounts of supporting evidence, whether biblical or extra-biblical, for some of the disciple's deaths over others, the idea remains true. They were friends of Jesus because they were willing to lay down their lives for his name's sake. Oftentimes the disciple's deaths are used, as well they should be, to support the idea that Jesus was in fact who he said he was, but let us not overlook the intimate friendship that existed between him and his disciples. He sacrificed his life and they sacrificed their lives because they knew that "this is the very best way to love. Put your life on the line for your friends" (John 15:13 MSG).

Obedience

After the monumental statement dealing with sacrificial love, Jesus then delivered another targeted insight on friendship: "You are my friends if you do what I command you" (John 15:14). The Greek word for *friendship* here means "a friend at court." It describes that inner circle around a king or emperor. (In John 3:29, it refers to the "best man" at a wedding.) The "friends of the king" would be close to him and know his secrets, but they would also be subject to him and have to obey his commands.[8]

So what does obedience to the words of Jesus have to do with friendship? Everything. You see, your inner circle is not a group of friends who sit around and look at *each other* asking tough questions; rather, your inner circle of friends should surround *King Jesus* and focus on his desires and commands. This is where most inner circles break down; they are egocentric rather than Christo-centric. They start with man's needs and thoughts instead of God's desires and thoughts. Part of our responsibility as friends is ensuring that the other members of our community are listening to the right voice and looking to the right person, Jesus.

Communication

Moses' meetings with God provide for us a basic insight into communication that should occur in friendship. "The LORD used to speak to Moses face to face, as a man speaks to his friend" (Exodus 33:11). The phrase "face to face" refers to a oneness and friendship within which clear communication takes place. Now, the Bible doesn't tell us, but I seriously doubt that Moses spent the majority of time talking. I mean, after all, he was meeting with God, and that is a pretty good time to shut the ol' yapper and listen. In fact, it is a good rule of thumb to listen twice as much as you talk.

Most people want to speak, or maybe they just want to be heard. Either way, it elevates their ego. Filling silence with stories or conjecture just for the purpose of being heard is not healthy communication. In the context of friendship, communication is conversation in which each individual is heard and the other is an interested listener. The conversation may be heavy in subject or more lighthearted, but in either case the communication should be edifying. Because the ability to care for one another's soul will require face-to-face segments of time in atmospheres that allow open and clear communication to take place.

Self-control

Scripture gives us a strong warning against being friends with people who have a hot temper they cannot control. The writer of Proverbs spoke of a man "given" to anger: "Make no friendship with a man given to anger, nor go with a wrathful man, lest you learn his ways and entangle yourself in a snare" (22:24–25). This is an individual who is not in control over his own moods; rather, he lets his mood master him. Because these types of people have no control over their temperament and words, they attack and destroy others as they go. The last part of the text warns that whoever is friends with this person may become entangled and also be enslaved by negative emotions. It may be said that this text teaches us a hot temper can be contagious. I have discovered in my own journey that those who let their emotions rule them are infectious individuals. If a good or bad attitude is in fact contagious, then we are to place ourselves around those who demonstrate self-control.

Paul spoke of self-control when he wrote, "God gave us a spirit not of fear but of power and love and self-control" (2 Timothy 1:7). The word *spirit* means one's demeanor or attitude; thus, the ability to control oneself characterizes what a follower of God should look like. It is a process to become the type of person who isn't held hostage by feelings or circumstances. The process includes a steady dose of experiencing Scripture personally and within the context of community. A life of self-control is governed by that which truly matters, and this can only be understood by knowing truth and being in healthy friendships. When we make it our priority to focus on these two elements—Scripture and community—then the desires of God become the filters for our emotions. And when the desires of God are the filters for our emotions, we become people not given to wrathful and hot-tempered tendencies.

Character

When a piece of iron is rubbed against another piece of iron, it shapes and sharpens it. Our friendships should make us better and we should make others better. "As iron sharpens iron, so a man sharpens the countenance of his friend" (Proverbs 27:17 NKJV) is a statement the writer of Proverbs made in the larger context of money and mutual help. Bible commentator John Phillips described how this verse deals with character:

> Underlying all true prosperity is integrity of character and scrupulous honesty in dealings with other people. Our friends and partners are important. We learn from one another; we take character and color from one another. Our character eventually shows in our faces.[9]

I like to think of this text as one of those summary statements to describe the entirety of a friend's interaction. Through the course of our relationships, we are constantly being shaped and modeled more and more to look like Jesus. We interact in such a way that our friends become a better version of themselves and it is obvious for others to see. Certainly the text helps us understand that the better version of ourselves is a result of enlightening interaction where our ideas and thoughts are challenged and strengthened. It is a worthy goal, to be sure, to strive toward becoming the type of friends who interact in such a way that we become better vessels for God to use. That's what character in action looks like—a piece of iron sharpening another piece of iron, so that each are of better use and are consistent with their purpose.

As doctors and patients—caregivers and care takers of each other's souls—may we be rooted and built up in the faith. Friendships cannot be taken for granted and must be seen as essential, so cultivate them in your own lives by focusing on developing the characteristics above. As we have seen, when true friendship occurs, so does accountability. So build friendships in which you minister and are ministered to with the hope of seeing Jesus one day. May we never look at each other and utter those haunting words Viktor Frankl heard in a concentration camp so many years ago: "You, too, are getting out?" Instead, let us make the decision that he made, never to leave a countryman behind.

CHAPTER THIRTEEN

COLLABORATION: WE > ME

A ny one person can change the world, but he or she cannot do it alone. One person will usually be the conduit through which an original vision or idea flows, but it will take a group effort to put it into action and see it come to fruition. In 1982, Jim Kouzes and Barry Posner, both professors of leadership at their respective institutions, began a landmark study to discover the best practices of leaders when they were at their personal best. They conducted volumes of quantitative and qualitative research through surveying, case studies, and interviews. The result was what they referred to as "The Five Practices of Exemplary Leadership," which would be unpacked in *The Leadership Challenge*, a book considered to be a modern-day classic and arguably the most trusted research ever in the field of leadership. Why do I bring this up? Because one of their findings stated that extraordinary leaders enable others to act by fostering collaboration and strengthening the members of a team.[10]

We have seen the characteristics or qualities of a healthy friendship, and now we will look at another type of relationship— one fueled by collaboration. I love this principle of leadership and ministry taught to me by one of my mentors, Dr. Jay Strack: "All of us are smarter than any one of us." I guess somewhere along the way the idea that we can accomplish more together than any individual can do on his or her own took root in my mind, and collaboration became an assumed part of my thinking. When I use the term *collaboration* or refer to collaborative relationships, I simply mean the willingness to partner with likeminded individuals, communities, and organizations to accomplish a common cause.

Every person with a sacred intent approach to life wants to accomplish more, not less, with the amount of time and energy they have been granted. In other words, we want our lives to matter, to be alive with purpose, and to make this world somehow better because we live in it. To accomplish more, maybe even something extraordinary, we need to be able to collaborate. Kouzes and Posner concluded, "Leadership is not a solo act, it's a team effort. In the thousands of cases we've studied, we've yet to encounter a single example of extraordinary achievement that's occurred without the active involvement and support of many people."[11]

The Scriptures are full of examples of collaboration. Our Lord chose to have a group of disciples play a strategic role in accomplishing his great cause of seeking and saving the lost (Luke 19:10). I am not suggesting that a disciple could rescue people from their sins, but no one can deny that our Savior's cause became the great purpose of the disciples' lives. Consequently, because the disciples collaborated with God's great rescue plan for humanity, disciples throughout history have continued to do the same—including us modern-day disciples. When Jesus sent out his disciples, he partnered them together. Luke 10:1 reads, "After this the Lord appointed seventy-two others and sent them on ahead of him, two by two, into every town and place where he himself was about to go." Why was it so important that they were partnered together? Because Jesus knew they would be stronger as a team than as individuals.

This is again reinforced in Ecclesiastes 4:12: "Though one may be overpowered by another, two can withstand him. And a threefold cord is not quickly broken" (NKJV). Not only did the disciples collaborate in serving Jesus—and Jesus fosters a culture of collaboration with *all* his followers—but Paul too always traveled and ministered with a team. Or consider the Old Testament examples of Moses and Aaron, Joshua and the Israelites at Jericho, David and Jonathan, Naomi and Ruth, and of course Shadrach, Meshach, and Abednego standing together in civil disobedience while honoring God.

One of my favorite examples of collaboration in the Old Testament is the story of Nehemiah leading the effort to rebuild the walls in Jerusalem. Upon hearing the news that his homeland was in disarray, Nehemiah left the comforts of the king's court to return home. Immediately upon his arrival, he assessed the crumbled walls and the burned-down gates. Nehemiah's solution was to assign a different portion of the wall to each family. Through this incredible exercise of collaboration, the wall was rebuilt in just fifty-two days. Nehemiah 4:6 reads, "So we built the wall. And all the wall was joined together to half its height, for the people had a mind to work."

Imagine if you were Nehemiah, and after a long and weary journey you at last arrived in your homeland. But when you got there, the swell of heritage rising from the deepest parts of your being was deflated by the sight of rubble and ash. And what made matters worse was that everyone had grown comfortable with the rubble. The walls had been down for so many years that people had assumed they would always be torn down. Looking across the city, seeing scenes of crumbled stone with vegetation growing in and around every crack, would you have envisioned a different day?

Scripture reports that Nehemiah one night imagined a fortified Jerusalem, surrounded by a wall that symbolically demonstrated God's promise and protection for his people. While everyone had grown comfortable with *destruction*, Nehemiah was thinking *construction*. His vision was, at this point, very simple: "Let's get the wall built." It would have taken Nehemiah the rest of his life to build the wall by himself, but together they accomplished the task in less than two months. Collaboration became the bridge from vision and imagination to implementation and actualization.

Collaboration is a powerful tool that can help any person or organization accomplish . . . well, more. With that in mind, the following is a list of benefits that come from fostering a collaborative spirit:

- Collaboration affords us the ability to multiply or expand our capacity rather than just striving toward an already existing capacity.
- Collaboration allows us to accomplish more without necessarily spending more time, energy, resources, or finances.
- Collaboration creates a shared risk with everyone involved, preventing any one person or organization from having all the skin in the game.

- Collaboration communicates to everyone collaborating, "We aren't afraid of others, and we place the greater good above individual gain."
- Collaboration exposes us to new relationships and audiences.
- Collaboration many times can serve as a preventative of an individual or organization becoming or appearing stale or stalled in their mission/cause.

Whether these benefits are applied to individuals or organizations, the point is that when we have a collaborative spirit, everyone involved wins. God is going to allow some of us to have big, audacious ideas and dreams that will change or even save many lives if they come to fruition. Let me assure you that God does want those ideas that please him to happen, but it's going to take the kind of collaborative spirit evident among Jesus and his disciples.

Finally, I want to provide a great example of collaboration. One of my favorite figures in recent history is Dietrich Bonhoeffer, the theologian/professor/pastor turned conspirator and spy. His was a short-lived life full of sacred intent that serves as an incredible example of teamwork for the purposes of justice.

Dietrich and his twin sister, Sabine, were born on February 4, 1906, into an affluent, aristocratic family. They were the sixth and seventh of eight children born to Karl and Paula Bonhoeffer, who lived in Breslau, Germany.[12]

The Bonhoeffers raised their children to be independent thinkers, a family trait that would serve Dietrich well throughout his life. Dietrich grew up in a home where emotionalism was not tolerated and one had to be able to articulate, defend, and act upon one's beliefs. He was trained not only to think clearly but to prove his thoughts *in action*. If he were unprepared to live out what he claimed to believe, perhaps he did not believe what he claimed after all. So from an early age Dietrich knew that ideas were never just ideas but the foundations on which he could build his actions and ultimately his life.[13]

Astonishing as it may sound, Dietrich declared at thirteen years old that he would become a theologian. True to his word, he left home to attend university in 1923 at the age of seventeen. Bonhoeffer would emerge from his formal education with a tension that he would carry with him the rest of his life, one between the church and the academy. Therefore, much of his professional career found him operating in both arenas.

Between 1932 and 1933, Nazis had risen to power in an extraordinarily short amount of time, and on January 30, 1933, Adolf Hitler was democratically elected chancellor of Germany. Bonhoeffer described this time as "a spectacle of a civilized society disintegrating into barbarism."[14] On March 20, 1933, Dachau was opened, the first concentration camp designed to hold political prisoners. Dachau would serve as a model for future concentration camps and as a "school of violence" for the SS (abbreviation for *Schutzstaffel*) under whose command it stood.[15] Hitler's campaign for complete control included incorporating Protestant youth organizations into Hitler Youth on December 20, 1933, and the political murders or blood purge of SA (*Sturmabteilung*, or Storm Troopers) leadership[16] between June 30 and July 2, 1934, including SA head Ernst Röhm.[17] On August 2, 1934, German President Paul von Hindenburg died and Hitler was proclaimed both chancellor and president.[18]

In 1938, Bonhoeffer joined a collaborative effort conspiring against Adolf Hitler and the Third Reich. The group included his older brother-in-law, Hans von Dohnanyi, who had served the Reich minister of justice, which allowed him "a blood-spattered front row seat at the inner workings of the Nazi leadership."[19] In February of that year, primarily through Dohnanyi, Bonhoeffer made contact with leaders of the political resistance made up of members of the Abwehr, the German Military Intelligence led by Colonel Hans Oster, who in turn reported to fellow conspirator and head of the Abwehr, Admiral Wilhelm Canaris.[20] Bonhoeffer's closest relationship in the conspiracy against Hitler would be Dohnanyi, who gave him information, advice, and eventually assignments.[21]

While Dohnanyi worked for the Ministry of Justice, he kept secret files of Nazi crimes, later to be known as the "Zossen files" or "chronicle of shame."[22] The atrocities that Dohnanyi chronicled included murders and attempted murders in the concentration camps, currency marketeering, corruption in the Hitler Youth and among SA leaders, speeches by Hitler, reports on treatment of prisoners, film of the atrocities in Poland, and much more. As his wife, Christine, worded it, "There was hardly an offense that wasn't listed in this Chronicle."[23]

The files also included details concerning the extent and duration of the collaboration and conspiracy against the government.[24] The files dated back to 1938, and since Bonhoeffer was part of the conspiracy in the Abwehr,[25] there is no reason to believe he was unaware of the atrocities that were being committed by the Third Reich. Eric Metaxas supported this when he wrote in his best-selling book *Bonhoeffer*, "Much of this information collected by Dohnanyi found its way to his brothers-in-law and their families. Before others in Germany knew of them, the Bonhoeffers heard of the mass murders in Poland, the systematic burning of synagogues there, and much else."[26]

On September 22, 1944, a Gestapo criminal investigator discovered Dohnanyi's secret archive of Nazi atrocities in the Armed Forces High Command outpost in Zossen.[27] Bonhoeffer was shortly thereafter linked conclusively to the conspirators and transferred to the Gestapo prison at the Reich Central Security Office.[28] The discovery of the Zossen files led to more arrests, including Dietrich's brother Klaus and his best friend, Bethge.[29] These arrests caused Bonhoeffer to forego an opportunity to escape for fear that retaliation might be taken on those close to him.[30] Along with other important prisoners, he was transported from the Reich Central Security Office prison to the Buchenwald concentration camp on February 7, 1945.[31] At the same time, Admiral Canaris, the former head of the Abwehr office and coconspirator of Operation 7 (named for the number of Jews initially involved in the mission), was taken to Flossenbürg.[32]

Bonhoeffer was again transferred, this time to Regensburg on April 3, and again on April 6 to Schonberg, before being moved the night of April 8 to Flossenbürg concentration camp.[33] He, along with Canaris, Oster, and coconspirators Sack, Strunck, and Gehre, was hanged the following morning from the Flossenbürg gallows; Dohnanyi was executed the same day in Sachsenhausen.[34]

The camp doctor who observed Bonhoeffer's death wrote ten years later:

Through the half-open door in one room of the huts I saw Pastor Bonhoeffer, before taking off his prison garb, kneeling on the floor praying fervently to his God. I was most deeply moved by the way this unusually lovable man prayed, so devout and so certain that God heard his prayer. At the place of execution, he again said a short prayer and then climbed the steps to the gallows, brave and composed. His death ensued after a few seconds. In the almost fifty years that I worked as a doctor, I have hardly ever seen a man die so entirely submissive to the will of God.[35]

All of Bonhoeffer's official training prepared him for the roles of theologian and pastor. Yet, unable to sit idly by while a madman ruled his country, he entered into collaborative relationships for the purpose of conspiring against Adolf Hitler's regime. The group would come close on at least one assassination attempt. But in the end, Bonhoeffer and his coconspirators died a gruesome death with the knowledge that Hitler was still alive and held up in a bunker with Allied forces closing in. I find it interesting that this collaboration was so upsetting to Hitler that, even as his world was crumbling around him, he still found time to order their execution as one of his final commands.

Each benefit that comes from a collaborative effort, which I outlined earlier, can be seen in this network of conspirators. While their ultimate objective was not met through their efforts, the collaborative spirit, and particularly the Zossen files, served to prove the justness of the cause. They collaborated because it was right, because their cause was just, and because passivity was not an option.

———

Through research evidence and biblical basis for collaboration, the practical benefits, and a real example from recent history, I hope you will become convinced in the power of what *we* can accomplish, as opposed to just *me*. May you begin to see collaboration as the fertile garden in which great ideas can be planted and grown. Or maybe collaboration will simply be the bridge to your engagement. In any case, my desire is that you realize the world can be changed—but not by one person acting alone. Because in the end, We > Me.

MOTIVATIONS

INTRODUCTION

INVISIBLE LABOR

CHAPTER FOURTEEN

I AM A GIANT KILLER

CHAPTER FIFTEEN

I'M ON AN ADVENTURE

INVISIBLE LABOR

S aturday is a great day for thinking and reflecting. At Easter, it is the day of silence sandwiched between Good Friday and Resurrection Sunday. As such, I want us to think about what motivates a life of sacred intent. In Victor Hugo's masterpiece *Les Misérables*, the character Cosette says, "A man is not idle because he is absorbed in thought. There is a visible labour and there is an invisible labour."[1] Invisible labor motivates our lives as well as determines the authenticity of our visible labor. In other words, an example of invisible labor was described by the apostle Paul when he wrote, "Finally, brothers, whatever is true, whatever is honorable, whatever is just, whatever is pure, whatever is lovely, whatever is commendable, if there is any excellence, if there is anything worthy of praise, *think* about these things" (Philippians 4:8, emphasis added). But an example of visible labor would be the very next verse, which reads, "What you have learned and received and heard and seen in me—practice these things, and the God of peace will be with you" (v. 9). To "think on these things" is the invisible labor that spurs on the visible labor of "practice these things" as an authentic action that allows us to enjoy the peace of God.

With that in mind, we turn our attention to the motivations

of a life filled with sacred intent. While a very long list of motivating factors could be articulated, my desire is to simplify provocation into two categories. First, because of what Christ has accomplished in our lives through salvation, we can live a triumphant life that includes "killing off everything connected with that way of death: sexual promiscuity, impurity, lust, doing whatever you feel like whenever you feel like it, and grabbing whatever attracts your fancy" (Colossians 3:5 MSG). Let's be honest, the things that are "connected with that way of death" can become giants in our lives that must be defeated.

Second, since Christ affords us the ability to live free from fear of the giants we face, we can then see life as a beautiful adventure. The adventure that is our lives finds its understanding and guidance in truth. Thus we will discover that we are guided by an ancient confession that captures the very essence of our Christian faith. We are adventurists bound together by the grace of God known as the church.

In the end, we are more than conquerors in Christ and part of the daring adventure of people following him. These are the two greatest motivations for every life full of sacred intent. And while these motivations cannot be seen or even heard, all those around us will feel the consequence of their impact. A life that is rightly motivated is rightly focused. A life that is rightly focused is full of obedience. A life that is obedient can engage and finish the adventure with a full measure of confidence and approval from his or her heavenly Father. So let us begin the all-important task of understanding the invisible labor that is motivation.

CHAPTER FOURTEEN

I AM A GIANT KILLER

To live a life full of sacred intent involves doing battle with the "old man" or "the flesh," as the apostle Paul referred to them. As you probably know, following Jesus does not mean you are exempt from temptations or a wide variety of struggles. Battling with these distractions is not something we can just check off our list. We do not attend a conference, read a book, or pray a prayer and then . . . *Poof!* . . . all the bad things disappear! God the Father and Jesus are not equivalent to Aladdin's genie in the lamp, nor is the Holy Spirit a fairy who helps you out when you wish upon a star. God has not revealed himself as a superhero who shows up to rescue us every time we are in trouble. Rather, God says that he is always with us, present in the daily comings and goings of life, whether they are stamped "routine" or "urgent." Because he is ever-present and all-knowing, God knows our needs even before we ask him (Matthew 6:8). Our great privilege is that we can "draw near to the throne of grace, that we may receive mercy and find grace to help in time of need" (Hebrews 4:16). Because God knows our needs in advance, and because he is always present to offer grace in times of need, we can claim the truth that "in all these things we are more than conquerors through him who loved us" (Romans 8:37).

To be a conqueror means that because of the love of Jesus, we can have overwhelming victory in our lives when facing all kinds of troubles. So in this chapter we will identify five struggles or temptations in life that must be overcome to experience a life of sacred intent. Make no mistake: an issue may at first appear small and insignificant, but left alone—that is, allowing it to exist in your life—each can grow into a giant that becomes all consuming, intent on devouring every bit of joy and happiness in life.

As a result, we must see ourselves as overcomers, as those who can battle the giants of life and emerge victorious in Christ. Just as David gathered five smooth stones, so I have identified five giants that must be killed, in some cases over and over again. Three steps are obvious concerning David's battle with Goliath: he was prepared, he was quick to act, and he aimed to kill. My hope is that by identifying these behemoths, we would become prepared to do battle, that the very existence of these giants would cause us to act quickly, and that we would aim to destroy their existence in our lives.

One last thing about David that I find fascinating: he was the only one who saw himself as a giant killer. When he stepped out on that field to face Goliath, armed only with a slingshot and a pouch of five stones, he did so fully convinced and fully confident in God's sufficiency. God was with him, God was protecting him, but David had to fight the colossus.

As a Christ follower, you are a giant killer because God is present within you. God is with you, God is for you, God will protect you . . . but you must step onto the battlefield yourself. No one can make you do battle with a giant, but God didn't call you to be a spiritual pacifist sitting on the sidelines hoping the giant won't notice you. Instead, God is present and sufficient, thus you can fight and emerge victorious.

> Then he took his staff in his hand and chose *five smooth stones* from the brook and put them in his shepherd's pouch. His sling was in his hand, and he approached the Philistine . . . When the Philistine arose and came and drew near to meet David, David ran quickly toward the battle line to meet the Philistine. And David put his hand in his bag and took out a stone and slung it and struck the Philistine on his forehead. The stone sank into his forehead, and he fell on his face to the ground. (1 Samuel 17:40, 48–49, emphasis added)

GIANT #1: PRIDE—*THE DISEASE OF ME*

Pride may be the ugliest sin known to be committed by mankind. Now, to be clear, there are two kinds of pride "a reasonable or justifiable self-respect; or improper and excessive self-esteem known as conceit or arrogance."[2] The apostle Paul even used the term *pride* in a positive light when he wrote to the Corinthian Christians, "I am acting with great boldness toward you; I have great pride in you; I am filled with comfort. In all our affliction, I am overflowing with joy" (2 Corinthians 7:4). For our purposes, we are referring to the second, sinful kind of pride that C. S. Lewis called in *Mere Christianity* "the complete anti-God state of mind."

Pride leads to a desire for worshipping self instead of Jesus, seeking fame instead of influence, and embracing the applause of others instead of praising God. There are ten Hebrew and two Greek words used for pride in the Bible, and all refer to an overinflated view of self or a haughty exalted attitude. In short, a prideful attitude is the complete opposite of a humble spirit.[3] As you will discover with all five giants, pride can quickly become a dominating evil presence in our life, much like Goliath standing out in the valley shouting obscenities toward the army of Israel.

Hall of Fame coach Pat Riley called pride "the disease of me." Is it not amazing that the most significant giant we face is our sinful selves? The question really is, how do we stay humble? Or rather, how do we destroy the giant of pride in our own lives? I would like to offer a few suggestions for always striving to be what I have often heard Bob Goff refer to as *the next humblest version of you*:

- Have a healthy prayer life, because it's hard to think too highly of yourself when you are kneeling at the feet of Jesus.
- Live a life always ever mindful of grace, because it's hard to be the hero of your story when you realize that you are the chief of sinners.
- Always consider others first, because it's hard to become full of self when you are constantly serving others.

GIANT #2: SEXUAL IMMORALITY—*FLEE!*

Pompeii was an ancient Roman City near modern-day Naples, Italy. When Mount Vesuvius erupted on AD 79, Pompeii was destroyed along with its eleven thousand inhabitants and buried under volcanic ash. The city would remain frozen in time and undiscovered for the next fifteen hundred years. Since its discovery and excavation, we have been given insight into ancient Roman culture almost perfectly preserved for nearly one and a half millennia. The volcanic eruption covering the town must have happened suddenly because it preserved a dog cowering, a mother covering her baby, and many other "pictures" of a city with no time to react. Hundreds of objects and artifacts have been unspoiled, including artwork, jewelry, boxes, weapons, pipes, crematorium urns, and even a loaf of bread. Today one can walk the excavated city streets of Pompeii and witness firsthand how city life would have existed during biblical times.

While the excavation of Pompeii has uncovered numerous treasures, it also has unearthed what was a sexually immoral and depraved culture. There is little doubt that Pompeii was a city for the super rich, full of aristocrats and wealthy merchants. Pornographic artwork and paintings decorated the walls, depicting the most depraved scenes. Secret chambers have been discovered dedicated to acting out whatever one's fantasy may have been on a given day. The Pompeians were infatuated with Eros, the son of Aphrodite, which is evidenced through the artwork and architecture of the city. The motto of Pompeii was, "Enjoy life while you can for tomorrow is uncertain." Sexual activity was considered one of the greatest ways to enjoy and get the most out of life.[4] They were a people who lived to please self sexually and were bombarded with sexual images on a daily basis. Sound familiar?

I cannot imagine growing up in this culture. As someone who spends much of my time teaching and speaking to students, rarely a week goes by where a young man does not reach out to me to discuss his addiction to pornography. We live in a culture where women are depicted and reduced to sexual objects that exist merely for male satisfaction. Ours is an over-sexualized culture with images bombarding women and men at every turn—the checkout line at the grocery store, the explore page on Instagram, the pop-up advertisements on almost any Web site, billboards and movie posters, television, and even commercials. While women are mainly drawn to porn driven by narrative, whether viewed on a screen or read in an erotic novel, men gravitate more toward traditional visual pornography. In any case, both forms of pornography have thoroughly saturated our culture. The question is, what can we do about it?

The Scriptures are very clear when it comes to any kind of immorality. There is no room for strategy or negotiation. The follower of Jesus, when confronted with sexual images of any kind, should immediately locate the nearest escape route: "Flee from sexual immorality. Every other sin a person commits is outside the body, but the sexually immoral person sins against his own body" (1 Corinthians 6:18). Following Jesus may sometimes look like we are running from impure images wherever they might present themselves, when really we are just running to Jesus. When we look, lust, or touch in a sexual manner anyone outside of the sacred agreement of marriage, then we contradict the very reason for which our bodies were purposed. The grammatical structure of the beginning of the above text, "flee from sexual immorality," is in the present imperative. We are to have the habit of fleeing without delay or consideration.[5] The very hint of temptation should serve as a Do Not Enter sign for all Christians living with a sacred intent.

GIANT #3: DISTRACTION—*A CASE OF BLURRED VISION*

It is so easy to get a case of blurred vision in a social media–driven world. Some of you have all the notifications on your phones flipped to the on position, so there is scarcely a minute that goes by without information pinging your way. In just a few short years, the evolution of technology has transformed all of us into photojournalists, movie and food critics, travel consultants, activists, advice givers, and the list goes on and on. We are hash-tagged and geo-tagged. We like, share, post, comment, and consume more information and images than ever before in human history. Lying just beneath the surface of all our interactions are algorithms fast at work determining what or who we should like, wear, or purchase next. We are drowning in a sea of digital white noise with waves of new technology steadily washing over us with each new technology release and update.

Truthfully, there are thousands of benefits to living in what has been referred to as the New Media, Information, or Digital Age. I am in no way anti–social media or anti-technology. In fact, I would argue that the benefits can far outweigh the drawbacks; nevertheless, there is a caution to be heeded. All the forms of communication and information can, if we are not careful, distract our focus from that which matters most.

I'm not saying that I have this all together, that I have it made. But I am well on my way, reaching out for Christ, who has so wondrously reached out for me. Friends, don't get me wrong: By no means do I count myself an expert in all of this, but I've got my eye on the goal, where God is beckoning us onward—to Jesus. I'm off and running, and I'm not turning back.

So let's keep focused on that goal, those of us who want everything God has for us. If any of you have something else in mind, something less than total commitment, God will clear your *blurred vision*—you'll see it yet! Now that we're on the right track, let's stay on it. (Philippians 3:12–16 MSG, emphasis added)

In the above text Paul wrote that he had his *eye* on the goal. Notice that he did not write, "I have my *eyes* on the goal." Other translations read speaking to focusing on one thing. In other words, Paul was expressing a singularity in his attention to the goal. So let us say it very clearly at this point: anything that detracts our focus from Jesus can and eventually will blur our vision. And when our vision is blurred, we cannot see clearly all that God wants for us.

Thus, the question we must wrestle with in our own lives is, do the different ways to communicate and assimilate information help or distract? Do they clarify things for us or just clutter the airways? Some of us should be asking ourselves if we are addicted to certain social media or feel the perpetual need to always have the latest and greatest available for purchase. Those with a sacred intent want all that God has for them, and what a tragedy it would be for that to get lost in the clutter of endless hashtags, 140-character messages, and obsession with double-taps. It is ironic that we live in an age where more can be consumed than ever before but that by consuming more, we may be receiving less of what God wants for us. Do not allow distraction to become the giant that blurs your vision.

GIANT #4: THE OLD MAN AND HIS PAGAN WAYS—*LIVING NEW*

While I was in college in the good ol' state of Tennessee, a few of my friends had the bright idea of driving across the country to California for our spring break. It seemed like a very naive, adventurous, college-like idea to just jump in the car and start driving. What could go wrong with four guys stuffed into a brown, 1978 Ford Pinto driving 2,180 miles and thirty hours one way, just to say we did? No one took into consideration that by the time we got to California, we would only have a few days to enjoy its sunshine and beaches before turning around to start the journey back to campus. Additionally, not one of us considered the ramifications of trying to drive a dilapidated, time-worn wreck that was older than the people behind the wheel.

Well, as any rational human being—present company *excluded*—may expect, the car did not quite make it. On the drive out, we broke down somewhere in the Rocky Mountains after ignoring warning signs and trying to drive through a frozen pass. Fortunately, we were able to get the car repaired by a friend of a friend in Denver, Colorado.

On our return home after enjoying a few days of sun and fun, the first thousand or so miles were rather uneventful as we enjoyed some of the most beautiful scenery between sea and shining sea. But then we hit the open fields of Kansas at about three o'clock in the morning. The car made some kind of sputtering noise before smoke started bellowing out of the hood like a brush fire that could not be controlled. So there we were in the middle of Kansas, in the middle of the night, in the middle of nowhere. The only option we could see was that two of us would jog to the next exit where hopefully we could find some help.

I volunteered for the job, as did my friend who had the nasty habit of smoking cigarettes. So there the smoker and I went, running down the highway into the dark abyss of cattle fields periodically interrupted by oil rigs. Soon our task became a burden too heavy for my friend's lungs to bear, and he began to get sick on the side of the road. Still, he was a trooper and soon carried on the best he could. We might have completed three or four miles before we heard the joyous sound of a vehicle on life support from somewhere behind us. Moments later the pinto emerged from the blackness and we jumped in without it even coming to a full stop. By the grace of God we made it to the next exit, where there was a truck stop with an all-night mechanic on duty.

His name was Larry, and when we entered the garage, he was asleep on a chair in the corner. His appearance was rough, and he looked as if he had not showered since . . . ever. It was forty-something degrees outside, and he was wearing a short-sleeved button-up shirt with his name embroidered on it. He felt the need to only utilize one of the buttons, providing us with a great view of his tattooed chest and "bowl extra full of jelly belly" hanging out beneath. When he awoke and stood to his feet, I noticed two tattoos across his knuckles, one said "love" and the other "hate." In a drunken haze he stumbled over to the pinto and lifted the hood. He proclaimed in a loud and surprisingly energetic voice, "Boys, it's broke!"

Needless to say, we were stuck and needed real help. We pooled our money and got a hotel room. The next morning a sober mechanic arrived and repaired the car. The pinto would break down once again, this time in Lexington, Kentucky. At this point we called a tow truck to haul us to Chattanooga, Tennessee, where a friend could then transport us back to college. Before the tow truck driver arrived, the four of us did the math and realized that only two of us could fit in the tow truck. We then devised a scheme that involved two of us hiding under some luggage in the pinto so we could all be carried to Chattanooga. You guessed it! Yours truly and the smoker would be in the pinto, loaded onto the truck, and illegally hauled down the road that night.

Like the Pinto, I used to be broke. I was lost in the middle of nowhere, stumbling around in the darkness. And to make matters worse, I had no way of helping myself. But then hope punched a hole in the dark abyss of nothingness and made a way for me. The glorious thing about the hope we have in Jesus is that he has the power to create, and that power is never more obvious than when he makes broken, dead people new. Most days my life is full of light, and the very moment at hand reminds me of this hope and God's grace. But there are those days when the darkness tries to creep back in and I am reminded that I was once broke and do not deserve the life I now enjoy. It is on those days the former broken-down version of me seems big and powerful—like a giant staring me down. J. C. Ryle wrote,

> True Christianity is a fight. He must fight the flesh. Even after conversion he carries within him a nature prone to

evil, and a heart weak and unstable as water. That heart will never be free from imperfection in this world, and it is a miserable delusion to expect it. To keep that heart from going astray, the Lord Jesus bids us, "Watch and pray."[6]

It is on those days, in the middle of a major battle, that I try to meditate with even more focus and energy on the greatest of realities that is at the very nucleus of sacred intent: we have been made new in Christ Jesus. Furthermore, and just as miraculous, we will never grow old again. The mercies of God are new every day, and every day is the day of salvation; therefore, following Jesus affords us the status of *new*.

We are the new creations that never become old creations. We can be eighty years old with the childlike joy of a new Christian bubbling out of us. We are new, and that is great news! The challenge we all face is to continually live new. The reason for this is because, though we are new, the old man and his pagan ways seems to live on like some kind of zombie looking to devour whatever is in its path. But take heart—the giant of our former, sinful selves has limited capacity and limited time. For there is coming a day when God will make all things new again. At that day and for all eternity, there will be a new heaven and a new earth. We will exist in a glorified state and in a glorified environment. What a magnificent day that will be! But until then we will face the giant that is our old flesh and go through the process of being sanctified so that one day "he might present the church to himself in splendor, without spot or wrinkle or any such thing, that she might be holy and without blemish" (Ephesians 5:27).

GIANT #5: A FALSE VIEW OF SUCCESS—
BIRDS CIRCLING THE DEAD

I used to think that success meant people recognized you and stroked your ego wherever you went. That successful people were obvious because of their money, possessions, authority, and status. We are trained to think that way, are we not? I mean, when you hear someone say, "She is enjoying a lot of success," we assume that achievement is obvious and glamorous. But what if success has nothing to do with money or power? What if it is something so altogether different that much of the world cannot even recognize it?

In Joshua 1:2–9, the Lord had a conversation with Joshua to give him instructions on how to lead now that Moses was dead. What is fascinating is that out of the ninety-two words that God spoke, forty-five of them had to do with keeping the law. We know the law today as part of the Bible. So the imperative at the center of God's discourse is to obey the law; that is to say, obey the Holy Scriptures. This would be the key to Joshua's success, and this is the key ingredient to our success today. God also said to be strong and courageous: "Only be strong and very courageous, being careful to do according to all the law that Moses my servant commanded you. Do not turn from it to the right hand or to the left, that you may have *good success* wherever you go" (Joshua 1:7, emphasis added). That seems to suggest that meditating on the Scriptures provides the necessary strength and courage that this young emerging leader would need.

I think a healthy understanding of success can be wrapped up in the phrase "obedience of faith," which the apostle Paul used to bookend Romans (Romans 1:5; 16:26). If success is simply obedience to God, then truly successful people are probably over-looked. They are most likely carrying on with their lives serving, working, building healthy families, and living with a sense of non-glamorous calling. Most likely they are not on anyone's "Top 100" list of the most influential leaders, and no one is clamoring to interview them. On any given Wednesday night they can be found playing an instrument in the praise band at church, coaching their kid's soccer team, or maybe even mentoring at an after-school program. They are successful while driving minivans, cramming for midterms, or picking up some extra hours at the factory to give their kids a better life.

For these successful people, the residue of calling saturates the seemingly mundane moments of their days. They are not looking for earthly recognition, and fame is a notion they want to remain foreign. Nor do they want to be the hero of their own story. They are perfectly content with not being in charge and have long since resigned from being CEO of the universe.

They are the successful ones—successful because they are obe-dient. They have killed the giant that says you need to be someone you are not. His carcass lies rotting on a field with the birds circling around as a victorious reminder that we all were created to bring attention to the name of Jesus, not our own.

I'M ON AN ADVENTURE

Have you ever wanted to go on an adventure? Men and women, boys and girls have always been drawn to adventurous endeavors throughout history. Some have only been casual observers, living vicariously through characters from a story communicated through a screen, book, stage, or that ancient thing called storytelling. These casual observers have limited experience because their adventures come only through observation, and usually by only two of the five senses—sight and sound. Casual observers may hear and see an adventure, but they don't ever get to experience it fully.

Then there are those who are not content with butter-saturated popcorn and oversized soft drinks as companions for a second-hand experience. These individuals assume the role of a character and consequently enter an adventurous story separate from the one they have been viewing. Make no mistake—they have a fuller experience because all five senses are engaged. They post selfies in different environments, usually making the same face. The appearance of adventure is enhanced through filtering the images and cropping the unwanted. The visual set of automatically location-pinned videos and pictures forever stands as hash-tagged artifacts of their experiences. They return from these adventures and say things like, "That was awesome! Where do you want to go and what do you want to do next year?" (or next month or next week).

But the individuals who engage all five senses do not have a cognitive grasp on the concept of adventure any more than the casual observer who engages just two senses. Both have diluted *adventure* into something that can be exhaustively planned and is usually relatively safe. They see it as something else to add to the resume of life experiences.

But I have come to understand adventure as anything but safe, and while one may determine the start, the adventure itself determines where the finish line exists. You see, I have enjoyed—and will continue to do so—being the casual observer where the adventure is as boxed in as the theater candy in my hand. Additionally, I have played the role of adventurous character on more than one occasion. Both were enjoyable. But at the end of the day, neither role is completely satisfying. They leave one wanting more because they are replicas or reflections of true adventure.

They shadow danger but, for the most part, are not intrinsically dangerous.

They shadow courage but mostly no bravery is required.

They shadow importance but rarely are a catalyst to change.

They shadow companionship but do not achieve deep intimacy.

They shadow diversity but never move from observing to experiencing.

They shadow uncertainty while the outcome can easily be predicted.

True adventure emerges from the shadows as something different from what we have previously known. Adventure is not safe but rather dangerous and potentially deadly, it consumes as much as it gives, and it's never predictable. And when the adventure is over, people do not say things like, "Let's do that again!" There are no selfies, no filters, and the pain and unpredictability cannot be cropped out. Now, do not get me wrong; when it is survived, it is invaluable. Adventure chews you up and spits you out. Like Jonah being vomited onto a beach at an originally undesired destination, so adventure will spit you out smelling terrible and heading a different direction. And though it was not originally desired, it feels designed. And therein lies the oddity of adventure: once you arrive at the destination, you feel as if you were intended to arrive there all along.

EVERY ADVENTURE HAS A STARTING POINT

If every adventure has a beginning, then the genesis of ours should always come from a concern for the movement of Christianity and the global church—basically every believer, both past and present, who is or has been part of the movement of Christianity. It is interesting to me that the term *catholic* comes from the Greek *katholikos*, meaning "throughout the whole" and "general."[7] Thus, when Ignatius, who was a student of the apostle John and the third bishop of Antioch, said, "Wherever Jesus Christ is, there is the catholic church," he was speaking to the universality of the church. Dietrich Bonhoeffer wrote in his doctoral thesis, "Where the body of Christ is, there Christ truly is. Christ is in the church-community, as the church-community is in Christ (1 Corinthians 1:30; 3:16; 2 Corinthians 6:16; Colossians 2:17; 3:11). 'To be in Christ' is synonymous with 'To be in the church-community.'"[8]

The church is beautiful and mysterious and indestructible. It's the kind of idea that one can lose hours thinking about. It is amazing to think of how people from cultures and language groups all over the world throughout time and history are actually bound together as one, for which Christ died. It was upon Peter's confession of faith that Christ said, "I will build my church, and the gates of hell shall not prevail against it" (Matthew 16:18).

Every adventure that is worth taking should contribute to the health and advancement of Christ's church. Isn't it great to know that the story of your life is actually woven together with those of millions of other Christians across the world and throughout time to create a much greater story—the story of God's people? A life full of sacred intent both understands and is motivated toward this end. Examples of adventure can range anywhere from building families to building organizations, partnering with great causes to planting churches, meeting physical needs to marching for social justice. Any one of these things may seem predictable and safe at first glance, but I assure you these adventures are not. I have met families and looked into the eyes of parents who have lost children, seen the scars of those who have stood for justice, and witnessed the rejection of a church planter who gave blood, sweat, and tears to a city.

Every adventure has a starting point. Ours is the church, the invisible church, the one that doesn't have a street address but rather is the culmination of all the adventures and stories that constitute Christianity.

EVERY ADVENTURE HAS A "BIG IDEA" THAT GUIDES

The big idea at the heart of our adventure dates back to before AD 250 with the formation of the Apostles' Creed. Legend has it that each of the apostles contributed an article to a confession of faith, or rule of faith, known as a creed,[9] while others believe it simply affirms apostolic doctrine. In any case, the purpose of the creed was to be a clear statement concerning what the church believed, thus protecting it from heresy. The term *creed* comes from the Latin *credo*, meaning "I believe." Therefore, a creed is really a statement of belief and acknowledgement of personal trust in God[10] that is to be affirmed by individuals and groups who profess to follow Jesus. The Apostles' Creed reads as follows:

> I believe in God the Father almighty, maker of heaven
> and earth;
> and in Jesus Christ his only Son our Lord,
> who was conceived by the Holy Spirit, born of
> the Virgin Mary,
> suffered under Pontius Pilate, was crucified, dead, and
> buried:
> he descended into hell; the third day he rose again from
> the dead;
> he ascended into heaven, and sitteth on the right hand
> of God the Father almighty;
> from thence he shall come to judge the quick and
> the dead.
> I believe in the Holy Spirit; the holy catholic church;
> the communion of saints; the forgiveness of sins;
> the resurrection of the body, and the life everlasting.[11]

When we as believers verbalize this creed, we are essentially demonstrating with our words an affirmation of our faith. Another way of looking at this creed is how it affirms the grand narrative that is God's story. God's story can be understood in these four parts, or plot movements:

1. God created everything and it was perfect and good.
2. Mankind rebelled against God's desires for his creation and thus needed to be redeemed.
3. God sent his only son Jesus to die on the cross and redeem mankind from his sins.
4. One day God will restore his creation and make all things new, but until that day the church will seek to fulfill God's desires and advance his mission.

In other words, this creed is a concentrated effort to affirm the good news that is the gospel of Jesus. This is the idea that should guide, or rather keep our focus, on any adventure.

EVERY ADVENTURE HAS A DESIRED GOAL

My desired goal is to tell a story that is an observation of this faith or creed in action. Ours is a belief not bound by borders or tradition but defined by the beautiful oneness of the church. Ours is an adventure *of* faith and *into* faith. As such, it cannot and will not be tamed—and one day we will all have the scars to prove it. My hope is that in the end you will discover your part of this greater adventure, even as millions of others do the same in their own way. May you be convinced that we have not been called to protect the church but build and advance God's cause through it. And finally, I hope you see that the bigger story of which you are a part cannot be contained and has no borders, for the supernatural doesn't fit in boxes made by human hands. Maybe what I want more than anything else is to invite you out of the shadows and into the adventure that is the marvelous light.

Every adventure has a starting point, an idea that guides, and a desired goal. The question that all of us who desire to live with sacred intent must answer is quite simply, "Is my story an adventure that is saturated with the mission of God?" You were created for story, adventure, mission. And one of life's greatest missteps would be to settle for simulation when you were intended for a dirt-underneath-your-fingernails experience. Helen Keller once wrote, "Life is either a daring adventure or nothing at all." We can either live or die, but to live is to engage adventure.

One of my favorite movies is *Hook* directed by Steven Spielberg. The movie stars the late Robin Williams as Peter Banning, an adult who is a husband and father of two children who has forgotten that he was once Peter Pan. Through a series of misfortunes while visiting Granny Wendy in London, Williams's character is taken back to Neverland to save his two kidnapped children from Captain Hook. The entire movie focuses on Peter Banning rediscovering his identity through the adventure of saving his children. I think the story of *Hook* reflects the truth of Christianity. It is through adventure that we discover, or rediscover, our identity. Jesus was and is central to the mission of God; to be called to a relationship with Jesus is to be called to the adventure that is his mission. In the final words of the movie, Granny Wendy asks Peter, "So . . . your adventures are over." Peter replies, "Oh, no. To live . . . to live would be an awfully big adventure."

SUNDAY

DREAMING

INTRODUCTION

A PERFECT DAY FOR
THE IMPOSSIBLE

CHAPTER SIXTEEN

THE DAY MACK THE TURTLE
BOLDLY BURPED

CHAPTER SEVENTEEN

TO CHANGE THE WORLD

A PERFECT DAY FOR THE IMPOSSIBLE

Sunday is the perfect day for believing the impossible. The resurrection of our Lord makes some of the apostle Paul's more memorable statements all the more believable and plausible: "I can do all things through him who strengthens me" (Philippians 4:13) and "Now to him who is able to do far more abundantly than all that we ask or think, according to the power at work within us, to him be glory in the church and in Christ Jesus throughout all generations, forever and ever. Amen" (Ephesians 3:20–21). The empty tomb forever exists as the greatest reminder that "with God all things are possible" (Matthew 19:26). So why do so many of us dream at night of things we cannot remember while refusing to dream during the day of ideas that can turn the world upside down?

In chapter 1 we identified the gift of imagination in the creation narrative. Imagination was intended to be an expression of creative energy to fulfill God's purposes within the context of his creation. The challenge becomes taking this concept and making it applicable. In an effort to "prime the pump," let us consider a few questions:

- What will you do with your life to change the world for the better?
- How will you use the gift of creativity to imagine a different or redefined culture?
- How will you find creative answers to a question that most are unwilling to ask?
- Will you allow the story of your life to be a catalyst toward solutions regarding some of society's most appalling crises?

Want to change things? Then you will need a dream! A dream is an idea that is the product of creativity and imagination, serving to fulfill God's desires for God's creation. Willing to change things? Then welcome to a rich history of dreamers of the day. Sunday is a great day to imagine the impossible, to focus on the conviction and strategy necessary to change the world for the glory of God, and to become better equipped to move forward.

CHAPTER SIXTEEN

THE DAY MACK THE TURTLE BOLDLY BURPED

Stories are a big part of the culture of our home. We tell, read, watch, act, and generally have a great time learning from and enjoying stories. This means that my kids have been introduced to the artistry of American cartoonist and writer Theodor Geisel, better known to millions around the world as Dr. Seuss. Each one of my children have a favorite Dr. Seuss story that I read to them while trying to use a variety of voices in an effort to bring the stories to life. Honestly, I think if Mr. Geisel were alive today and could observe my impressions and shenanigans while reading his classics, he would probably laugh and say something like, "Thanks, but no thanks—you are not helping." My son Gabriel's favorite Dr. Seuss story is a work entitled *Yertle the Turtle*, which was published in 1958.

The story takes place on the Island of Sala-ma-Sond, where a turtle named Yertle serves as the king of a particular pond. In the beginning of the book everything is great on the pond. The other turtles enjoy a good, clean environment with plenty to eat and all a turtle would require to live a happy life. Everything is fine—that is, until Yertle becomes unhappy with the smallness of his domain. At this point he says,

I don't see enough. That's the trouble with me.
With this stone for a throne, I look down on my pond
But I cannot look down on the places beyond.

So the Turtle King orders nine turtles to come to him, and he has them stack on his stone throne. Then he climbs on top of the stack and can see for almost a mile. Yertle honestly believes that if he can see it, then he rules over it. Such an overinflated view of one's own purpose and role in life creates a hunger that can never be satisfied. And so it was with the Turtle King.

Unsatisfied with only seeing about a mile, he orders two hundred turtles to stack up one on top of the other so that he can see about forty miles from his throne in the sky. At this point he shouts, "Hooray! . . . I'm the king of the trees! . . . For I am the ruler of all that I see!"

Every turtle in the pond is afraid of the Turtle King, and so they obey his command and stack one on top of each other. Well, until one turtle named Mack, who happens to be on the very bottom of the stack, expresses his displeasure and the pain it is causing him to be on the bottom of the pile. He voices his concerns more than once to Yertle, and each time Yertle shows how little he thinks of his subjects and quips back for Mack to shut his mouth.

Then the Turtle King notices the moon in the night's sky. True to form, Yertle orders that thousands of turtles be stacked up so that he can rule over this glowing thing in the sky. Mack has enough of the Turtle King's obsessive thirst for power. In fact, he gets mad at Yertle and the entire situation, and "that plain little Mack did a plain little thing. He burped! And his burp shook the throne of the king!"

Mack's bold burp shakes the entire stack of turtles at Yertle's feet. It shakes the stack so hard that Yertle falls off of his throne and all the way back down to the pond with a big *Plunk!* Mack has freed all of the turtles and would-be victims of the king. He has freed the pond from tyranny and dictatorship. In short, Mack could not continue being used as a pawn to feed the king's oppressive use of power. So the story ends with all the creatures being free, just as they should be.

Like many of Dr. Seuss's books, there is a political message, and if I had to sum up the meaning of *Yertle the Turtle* it would be that all deserve to be free from dictatorship and tyranny. But I wish to accentuate a different idea in the story. Changing the culture of the pond began with one turtle's unwillingness to tolerate injustice any more. The next chapter will look at how a dream can change the world, but for now we'll focus on understanding the need that precipitates the dream. Every dream begins with a need, thus dreaming begins not with "What if?" but with "What must change?" For Mack, the "What must change?" was the rule of Yertle the King.

Over the previous twenty years, tens of thousands of students have attended a series of conferences known as Student Leadership University, which also happens to be the ministry I serve. Our organization exists to give students a fifteen- to twenty-year head start on how to think, dream, and lead at the feet of Jesus. While much of what we teach has evolved and been changed over the years, one session has remained consistent year in and year out. It is the session on dreaming in which the students are asked a potentially life-changing question: What would you do with your life if you knew you would not fail?

I have had the amazing privilege to be present for the conception of literally thousands of dreams, all of which seek to change something about the world. Yet throughout all the years and all the dreams articulated, I have never heard one student proclaim their dream to be that the world or some aspect of culture would remain exactly as it is now. No person dreams of more of the same or writes down, "How can we keep things exactly as they are?" Why? Because dreams are not about preservation and maintenance; rather, they focus on vision and transformation.

Were it not for dreamers of our day, the present situation would be as good as it gets. Dreamers change things because, deep in their souls, they believe those changes are essential. In fact, dreamers believe that if they do not envision and lead change, circumstances will erode and worsen.

Now, Yertle was a dreamer, but he wanted more so that he could feed his insatiable, warped, and prideful ego. There are plenty of those who have ideas and visions absorbed with self, and their every thought marinates in vanity. These types of people need to be dethroned from their prideful perch because they make the world in general a bad place. But the very existence of these types of people raises the need for those who would envision and articulate God-glorifying dreams. Dreams that build up others, not self— and dreams motivated by need, not narcissism.

Therefore, if you wish to have a dream, if you would like the story you tell with your life to be a catalyst for changing the world for the glory of God, then you must have a life full of belief. By that I mean you must have a deep well of faith, or as Paul wrote in Colossians 2:6–7: "Therefore, as you received Christ Jesus the Lord, so walk in him, rooted and built up in him and established in the faith, just as you were taught, abounding in thanksgiving." A life with strong belief that is rooted and growing in truth is perfectly positioned for a dream. Dreaming begins with conviction, not imagination. For the remainder of this chapter, we'll focus on the three types of conviction that provide a necessary foundation for imagining a better world. These convictions are based on three terms or metaphors expressed in the scripture above that describe being steadfast in the faith: *rooted*, *built*, and *walk*.

STUBBORN CONVICTION: *ROOTED*

What does it mean to be deeply rooted in Christ Jesus the Lord? First, we need to note that the term *rooted* is in the past tense and points to our initial conversion when we "received" Christ Jesus the Lord. As Christians we have received Jesus into our lives, and this causes us to be rooted in the unshakable Rock that is our Lord. That we are rooted in Christ Jesus means ours is a conviction that can withstand any storm. Reformer John Calvin's description of the rooted metaphor is particularly helpful:

> For as a tree that has struck its roots deep has a sufficiency of support for withstanding all the assaults of the winds and storms, so, if any one is deeply and thoroughly fixed in Christ, as in a firm root, it will not be possible for him to be thrown down from his proper position.[1]

The psalmist wrote, "The righteous flourish like the palm tree" (Psalm 92:12). I live in Florida, where palm trees are as common as yellow cabs in New York. During our time living in the sunshine state, we have seen our fair share of storms and the occasional hurricane. We also have pine and oak trees in Florida, and when a severe storm or hurricane comes through, the pines can break like a toothpick and even the oldest oaks can get uprooted and destroyed. But the palm trees always remain. They can bend over double without breaking in hurricane-force winds and straighten back out with all the leaves still intact. Some even believe that enduring the storms make the palm trees stronger and healthier.

The question is, how can a palm tree withstand 145-mile-an-hour winds? The answer is found in its root system. A palm tree's root system is made up of a large number of short roots that spreads out in about two feet of soil. Because of the high volume of roots, it is able to grasp a lot of soil around the root ball, creating a very strong anchor. Additionally, the palm tree's flexible trunk and feather-like leaves enable it to survive the storms as well, but it is how the roots grab hold of the soil that may be its strongest characteristic. To put it another way, the palm tree's roots cannot be separated from the soil.

And so it is that when the Christian is firmly rooted, he or she cannot be separated from the soil that is the Savior. When we are "in Christ" the roots of our life are found in the gospel. We are planted in a love that refuses to let us go:

> For I am sure that neither death nor life, nor angels nor rulers, nor things present nor things to come, nor powers, nor height nor depth, nor anything else in all creation, will be able to separate us from the love of God in Christ Jesus our Lord. (Romans 8:38–39)

To have a stubborn conviction is simply to say that the gospel is the undeniable center of my life. We are afforded a stubborn conviction because of God's unfailing or stubborn love.

GROWING CONVICTION: *BUILT*

While the word *rooted* is in the past tense, *built up* is in the present tense and speaks to the present work being accomplished by the gospel in our lives. It is how we are being built up on the firm foundation of Christ's finished work on the cross. As a follower of Jesus, we are continually being built up. We have not arrived as a finished work that can then be put on display behind glass and toured around the world so that all can see a Christian who needs no further growth. In fact, there may be no better description of a Christian, young or old, than what I read on a sign the other day at a worksite: Under Construction.

There is a sacred correlation between being rooted in the faith and built up by it. The deeper or stronger one's roots, the more one can grow. It could be understood that the stronger the foundation, the more floors can be added to the building. If our lives are rooted in the gospel, then there are no excuses and we are called to grow. Yet, as amazing as it may sound, many of our lives appear as a beautifully laid foundation with only simple framing that has been collecting cobwebs for years. Ours should be a conviction rooted in Jesus and ever-growing to reach new heights. We should live life in such a way that our growth does not allow for cobwebs to form.

RELEVANT CONVICTION: *WALK*

The word *walk* is describing how we should behave according to biblical principles as we make our way through a broken and fallen world. The Christian life continues in the way it was begun, at the feet of Jesus. As we journey and grow in our faith, we will hold onto certain beliefs tightly and others loosely. As I grow in my faith, I hope to embrace the fundamentals of the Christian faith with every fiber of my being. But at the same time, I don't want the nonessentials to inform my thinking from the backseat. We should walk through this world allowing the primary aspects of our faith to be . . . well, *primary*. But let all else be important without dominating the airwaves. I think this is what it means to walk in Christ Jesus the Lord.

Paul was explicit in his description of Christ Jesus as "the Lord." The term for *Lord* is derived from a Greek word for might and power. The word Paul uses for Lord, which appears 748 times in Scripture, means "master, sovereign, and owner." Paul was communicating to the Christians in Colossae that Jesus was in charge of every facet of their lives and thus exhaustively relevant to all that would happen in life. If Jesus is to be relevant in my life, that means I allow the gospel to inform my thinking concerning culture and any issues that rise up.

Christians should have deep convictions about current events, whether they be politics at home or injustices on the other side of the planet. After all, you cannot change a world for the better without first understanding the narrative that led to its current state. There is a difference, though, between strong convictions and an overinflated view of your opinion. An opinion is only good for sharing and in the end will probably cause more harm than health. A conviction, however, is not an opinion shared from a soapbox but rather it is a deeply held belief based on a deeply held faith. Christians should understand the crises of this world, have a conviction about what needs to change, and be bold enough to fight for that change to come about.

Courage and compassion are both fueled by conviction, and those who follow Jesus should be full of conviction. Likewise, a great dream always envisions some sort of change in this world. But before we can have a dream, we need conviction and to be firmly rooted, being built up, and walking in Christ Jesus the Lord. The world is full of Yertles that need to be dethroned. Unfortunately, it seems the world needs a few more Macks willing to take action. It only takes a burp . . . that is, it only takes one person full of conviction. I guess the only question left to answer is, are you brave enough to be a Mack?

TO CHANGE
THE WORLD

There is an odd breed of individual who dares to look out a different window. They are the dreamers of the day, telling a story with the moments of their lives, all the while believing they can be used to accomplish the extraordinary. They allow their eyes to scan the landscape of history and are inspired by those who have accomplished the seemingly impossible, or at least the highly improbable. Today most people marvel at what Dr. Martin Luther King Jr., Abraham Lincoln, William Wilberforce, Dietrich Bonhoeffer, Billy Graham, Elizabeth Fry, Aleksandr Solzhenitsyn, and others accomplished in their lifetimes. Basically, they admire the history, what is in the past. Our dreamers, though, focus on the future, and they see these individuals as examples of possibility for us. They see greatness and opportunity where others just see a wonderful story that could be turned into a movie.

As we discovered in the last chapter, conviction is the foundation on which imagination can creatively construct a dream. To change the world often begins with what is considered at the time an insignificant moment or action. But next there must be a path, a way forward to accomplish abundantly more. We need a unified strategy—not a uniformed one—to see our dreams realized. Below

I present a cloud of witnesses, along with principles for establishing a unified strategy, that I hope will encourage you to imagine a better world and put your dreams into action.

DON'T LET OTHERS JUDGE YOU
BECAUSE OF OUTWARD APPEARANCES

Changing the world begins with a belief that God has blessed you with the ability and capacity to do so. God doesn't concern himself with an ever-growing list of reasons why others think you should not dream and lead. That list includes, but is not limited to

- Age (being too young or too old)
- Family background
- Lack of education
- Past mistakes or failures
- Color of one's skin
- A disability
- Sex
- Lack of experience
- Lack of resources

And the list could go on and on. The reason God is not concerned with these things is "the LORD doesn't see things the way you see them. People judge by outward appearance, but the LORD looks at the heart" (1 Samuel 16:7 NLT).

I am a big fan of education, but God has used and will continue to use people with a dream but no degree. I think families should be healthy and strong, but God uses people who were born into very unhealthy families. I believe no one should ever be oppressed due to their skin color or sex, yet some of the greatest dreams were born in the minds of those under oppression. I believe God wants us to live righteous and holy lives, yet God uses people with checkered pasts.

History is inundated with dreamers who were undeterred by others' lists of disqualifications. Abraham Lincoln was one of our greatest presidents and had only eighteen months of formal education. Elizabeth Fry served as a catalyst to change the entire prison system throughout England, Europe, and much of the world and she did so in a male-dominated society. Dr. Martin Luther King Jr. led a movement and aroused the consciousness of a nation in a mostly Caucasian-led culture. Fanny Crosby was blind from shortly after birth but still wrote over eight thousand hymns. God does not see us as disqualified from having a dream simply because of what others may think. He knows that he created each and every one of us with the gift of imagination. We are all artists purposed to compose a story with the lives we lead. Because we have the capacity for creativity, we have the ability to articulate a dream. The ability to conceive a dream is not reserved for those who fit a certain image, but rather for all who have been made in the image of God.

THE VISION MUST BE SIMPLE YET COMPELLING

Undoubtedly one of the great wartime leaders and wordsmiths of the twentieth century was none other than Sir Winston Churchill. There may have never been a more compelling speech, at a most desperate hour, than his first as prime minister of England. Churchill was sixty-six years old when he became prime minister, with several lifetimes' worth of accomplishments on his resume.

He was an award-winning writer, politician, decorated officer in the British army, historian, and artist. He had also been on the forefront of warning against the potential threat with the rise of the Nazi party in German politics.

Nevertheless, he would assume the role of prime minister believing it might be too late to stop Hitler and that the winner of World War II could soon be this madman bent on ruling the world.[2] Churchill was nominated for the position of prime minister the night of May 10, 1940, as Hitler's army was marching across Western Europe gobbling up countries at will. Historian John Lukacs noted that Churchill was not a religious person, "yet he believed that what had come to him that day was due to Providence of which he was but an instrument."[3] Churchill himself would later recall about the evening of May 10:

> As I went to bed about 3 a.m., I was conscious of a profound sense of relief. At last I had the authority to give directions over the whole scene. I felt as if I were walking with Destiny, and that all my past life had been but a preparation for this hour and for this trial.[4]

So it was on May 13, with Hitler winning the war, that Churchill entered the House of Commons to deliver his first speech. In addition to the pressures of the war, he also felt under attack within his own government, as he was not the first choice for prime minister and was rather unpopular with much of Parliament. Churchill's predecessor, Neville Chamberlain, who had resigned after misjudging Hitler and was still his party's leader, walked into the room first and was welcomed with cheering, shouting, and a heroic reception that lasted two long minutes. Next, Churchill entered the room to nothing more than a golf clap that was over almost as soon as it had begun.[5] He then proceeded to deliver one of his shortest speeches, intended to be a call to arms for the British government to wage war against Nazi Germany. The speech was 730 words in length, of which the first 495 were opening remarks and a progress report of the current situation. It was the last 235 words where Prime Minister Churchill turned up the heat and left an indelible mark in history:

> I would say to the House, as I said to those who have joined this government: "I have nothing to offer but blood, toil, tears and sweat."
>
> We have before us an ordeal of the most grievous kind. We have before us many, many long months of struggle and of suffering. You ask, what is our policy? I can say: It is to wage war, by sea, land and air, with all our might and with all the strength that God can give us; to wage war against a monstrous tyranny, never surpassed in the dark, lamentable catalogue of human crime. That is our policy. You ask, what is our aim? I can answer in one word: It is victory, victory at all costs, victory in spite of all terror, victory, however long and hard the road may be; for without victory, there is no survival. Let that be realised; no survival for the British Empire, no survival for all that the British Empire has stood for, no survival for the urge and impulse of the ages, that mankind will move forward toward its goal. But I take up my task with buoyancy and hope. I feel sure that our cause will not be suffered to fail

among men. At this time I feel entitled to claim the aid of all, and I say, "come then, let us go forward together with our united strength."[6]

Churchill's vision was clear: to wage war with every available resource and defeat Hitler's army. In just 235 words, he explained in simple and compelling language that things were going to get a lot worse before they improved; a lot of people were going to die before millions could live free. Likewise, his goal was well-defined and compelling: victory. In reading this speech, and with a retrospective view of WWII, I can understand why so many were willing to die for their freedoms. Churchill presented his vision as if it were the only plausible option available to the British people. And the final words served as an exclamation point for a unified government and country to rally to this cause: "come then, let us go forward together with our united strength." One almost gets the sense that Churchill was not delegating or even pointing the way, but rather saying, "Let's join hands." The visionary, the dreamer, must cast vision in such a way that others understand and feel the sense of urgency and need. It must be done in a manner that motivates all who are listening to join hands and sacrifice for the cause.

BE MORE FULL OF CAUSE THAN PHYSICAL STRENGTH

Many in Europe viewed David Livingstone as an explorer using the latest technologies available to discover the darkest corners of Africa. In reality, Livingstone saw himself as a missionary who explored for the purposes of bringing Christianity and civilization to unreached peoples. At first he desired to be a medical missionary to China, saving and studying so that he could attend and receive the necessary education. Then, in September 1839, the First Opium War began, thus closing the door for missionaries in China. Within six months he met a missionary named Robert Moffat, who had been very successful running a station on the coast of South Africa. In one of their initial conversations, Moffat encouraged Livingstone to explore new territory in Africa, explaining how he had looked "to the vast plain to the north of the mission station, where sometimes was seen by the light of the morning sun the smoke of a thousand villages, where no missionary had ever been."[7]

Moffat may have gotten more than he bargained for because Livingstone eventually married his daughter, Mary. The couple would have six children. After the death of one of their children, the couple realized the jungle life of a medical missionary was far too dangerous and Mary returned home to raise the children. David Livingstone's life was a narrative of heartache and gospel advancement. He would suffer physically and emotionally throughout his lifetime. He survived a lion attack that left him with only the use of one of his arms. He nearly starved on more than one occasion and survived for months on maize. He nearly drowned once in a swamp. Livingstone would get lost more than once on his explorations and was even abandoned at times by those who were supposed to help him.

When he finally did return home, he discovered that his father, who had inspired in him from an early age the stories of great missionaries, had just died. The brokenhearted missionary was hardly recognizable by his family. At one point he had walked into a tree limb that damaged his face and left one eye blind and the other scarred, and his skin had turned tough and leathery from overexposure in the African sun.

After some rest, he returned to Africa. Then one day his wife wrote to him that the children were now grown and she could rejoin him in being a missionary to the people of Africa. Sadly, Mary died from malaria after she finally arrived to be with her husband.

In his later years, when he no longer had the strength to chart new paths through the bush, he would be carried from village to village on a stretcher. At each stop he was placed in the middle of the village where he could share Jesus with all who would listen. When his body was failing and trembling from sickness and high temperatures, Livingstone requested that he be taken home. Two men who were helping him took him back to his room, where he then requested to be placed in a kneeling position by his bed. Out of respect and reverence the men left him for some time to be alone with God. When one of his national brothers returned to check on him, he discovered that David Livingstone had died kneeling before God. Evangelist and apologist Ravi Zacharias concluded of Livingstone, "He died exactly the way he lived, in the presence of his Lord."

It is impossible to assign a number to how many Africans have been converted to Christianity as a result of David Livingstone's faithfulness. His dream was that the smoke of a thousand villages would be illuminated with the gospel of Jesus Christ. This was a dream realized and actualized by a man dedicated to his calling from the year 1841 until his death in 1873. His cause was bigger than himself.

One individual may conceive the dream, but the dream itself

will always be bigger than one person. We must pursue our dream with a willingness to roll until the wheels fall off. We must be comfortable with this notion, realizing the cause was all along bigger than our personal strength.

THINK BIG, BUT START SMALL

In 1813, a missionary from France named Stephen Grellet visited one of the most deplorable and notorious places in London, Newgate prison. After convincing the prison authorities to separate the young boys from the older, more seasoned criminals, he visited the women's side of the prison, which was two long yards occupied by nearly three hundred women. While there, Grellet observed dying women lying on the bare floor or, if one was lucky enough, some old straw. Moreover, there were almost-naked babies who had been born in the prison and were crying with no one to offer them comfort from the cold January winter.[8]

Grellet's first thought after leaving the prison was to reach out to his friend Elizabeth Fry so that she might help the children who were in desperate need of warm clothes. Fry was a Quaker minister and preacher who had built quite a reputation for serving the less than fortunate. Upon hearing Grellet's description of the prison, Fry and her sister Hannah visited Newgate to investigate the scene for themselves. The women prisoners would press their bodies against the bars and stretch out their hands begging for a pence to spend on beer, which the prison kept on tap.[9] Those fortunate enough to be at the front would have to fight off the prisoners behind them who were willing to pull hair, scratch, bite, and literally claw their way to the front. Biographer Janet Whitney wrote of Fry's first impression of the prisoners at Newgate, "She had seen drunken Irish, gypsies in the extremes of poverty, the squalor of the London slums, but she had never seen before a mass of women, by the hundreds, reduced to the level of wild beasts."[10] One sight she observed that was particularly heartbreaking was when she saw two prisoners taking the clothes off a dead baby to clothe a live one.

Elizabeth Fry would soon thereafter focus her energy on reforming a broken system at Newgate prison. Early in the 1800s, prisons in England existed only to punish prisoners and cared little for the conditions they endured. Fry opposed such a view and saw prison as a place for reform and preparation to return prisoners to society as contributors. In many ways Elizabeth Fry was a woman of many firsts. She was the first person to start a school in a prison, the first to start a national initiative for women, the first woman to testify before Parliament, and much more. In short, Fry saw the infinite value in each prisoner and the potential person they could become.

Historian Henry Fielding referred to Newgate as a "prototype of hell," but Elizabeth Fry saw it as a laboratory where one could be redeemed and rediscover purpose. Many of the reforms she implemented are still in effect today in prisons all over the world, but it all began with a concern for one prison. Out of that prison emerged a template for reform that could be implemented in prisons in civilized societies worldwide. I heard the pastor of North Point Community Church, Andy Stanley, say in a sermon once, "Do for one what you wish you could do for everyone."

Big dreams usually never get off the ground because they cannot be immediately implemented at a macro level. The dreamer logs the idea away for some future time when the world is ready.

But maybe the problem is not with the dream but with the dreamer. We must be willing to implement and pursue our dream at a micro level, so that our dream can evolve to the point that it can be effective at a macro level.

We must be willing to reform one prison (or one person or one situation) and through the process create a system or unified strategy for even greater reform later. Want to change a state? Start with a city. Want to change education? Start with one school or, better yet, one class. Are you dreaming of a day when there will be no more poverty? Then feed the hungry people in your immediate area, and in so doing you will create a strategy that can be implemented in other cities. Want to do something to save music in schools? Then buy an instrument for a kid and teach him or her how to use it. In other words, do for one what you wish you could do for everyone, and in the process you may discover just how to do for *everyone*.

HAVE AN ECLECTIC GROUP OF ALLIES

One of the greatest examples of an eclectic group of people coming together for a cause took place with the election of Abraham Lincoln as the sixteenth president of the United States on November 6, 1860. There are few who would debate that Lincoln took office at one of the most volatile times in American history. Seven states in the South had seceded, forming the Confederate States of America following his election. That number would expand, and the Civil War would ensue from the years 1861 to 1865, leaving over six hundred thousand Union and Confederate soldiers dead. Upon entering his presidency, Lincoln believed he did so "with a task before me greater than rested upon Washington."[11]

The question was, what kind of an administration would he build in such an unstable and explosive time? What kind of a team would he assemble to help him move America toward the extinction of slavery? In many ways Lincoln had set the stage for the end of slavery in his "House Divided" speech that he gave in 1858 after being nominated for the U.S. Senate. In it he stated, "Either the opponents of slavery will arrest the further spread of it, and place it where the public mind shall rest in the belief that it is in the course of ultimate extinction; or its advocates will push it forward, till it shall become alike lawful in all the States, old as well as new— North as well as South."[12]

If Lincoln's chief aim, or dream, was the abolition and extinction of slavery, then it would require a uniquely qualified team. Therefore he made a decision very different from any of his predecessors when constructing his cabinet. In her award-winning book *Team of Rivals: The Political Genius of Abraham Lincoln*, Doris Kearns Goodwin wrote about the men who served on Lincoln's cabinet from 1861–65. Three of the men he appointed had just run against him in the 1860 campaign for office of the president. Lincoln had succeeded against more accomplished and better-educated rivals who had made all sorts of accusations against him through negative campaigning or mudslinging.

Yet realizing each of their strengths, he decided to put them in his cabinet and give them a role in his administration. Goodwin wrote, "It was this capacity that enabled Lincoln as president to bring his disgruntled opponents together, create the most unusual cabinet in history, and marshal their talents to the task of preserving the Union and winning the war."[13] In an effort to explain such a decision, Lincoln remarked, "We need the strongest men of the party in the Cabinet. We needed to hold our own people together. I had looked the party over and concluded that these were the very strongest men. Then I had no right to deprive the country of their services."[14]

To change the world you will need a team of people to rally around your dream. The temptation will be to collaborate with people who like you and think like you do. But there is strength in building a team that no one else would have ever thought to assemble. This is the secret we can learn from President Abraham Lincoln. A team of people with a wide variety of strengths and skill sets. A team that is full of different personalities and styles. A team that is rich with diversity and a wide range of assets. A team of rivals, an eclectic team, can change the world.

MAINTAIN A PATIENT DILIGENCE

To change the world will require a quiet strength, a patient diligence. Dreams that change things are often a slow burn illuminating the possibility of what could be. They require that old-fashioned thing that cannot be downloaded or outsourced: endurance. And so it was with the man who wore number 42 for the Brooklyn Dodgers from April 15, 1947, until his final at bat on October 10, 1956.

Jackie Robinson was the youngest of five in a family of share-croppers still living in the shadow of slavery in Georgia, known as the Jim Crow laws. His father left home early on, and Mallie Robinson raised her children to understand the "value of fam-ily, education, optimism, self-discipline, and above all, God. She saw to it that her children were in church on Sunday and taught them the value of prayer."[15] Mallie diligently saved her money and moved the children to Pasadena, California, in an effort to provide for them better opportunities for their future. She was a Bible-believing woman who raised her children to love their enemies and never repay evil with evil. Though young Jackie had a temper, the godly parenting of a single mother would lay a foundation for him to endure a storm of persecution on the not-too-distant-horizon.

Other mentors, such as a Methodist preacher named Karl Downs, would influence Jackie to control his anger and temper in the face of injustice through a deeper relationship with Jesus. During his time as a student at UCLA, Robinson lettered in four sports and won the National Collegiate Athletic Association broad jump title. After college he would play semiprofessional football for the Honolulu Bears before being drafted into the army in 1942.

Throughout his entire life, he faced racism. Though the Jim Crow laws of the South were nonexistent in California, prejudice was still very commonplace. Further still, the United States Army was quite segregated, and he still experienced discrimination from the stools at a soda fountain to the sports teams where Jackie was told he could not play with the whites. In 1944, he was honorably discharged, and shortly thereafter he briefly returned to football. He then became the athletic director for Sam Huston College before going to play baseball for a Negro National League team.

It was during this time that Branch Rickey, a Bible-believing Christian and the general manager for the Brooklyn Dodgers, was devising a plan to integrate baseball. Rickey felt that Robinson was just the man to break the color barrier. Eric Metaxas described Rickey's mind-set in choosing Robinson: "He had to be sure he was choosing someone who understood the tremendous import of not fighting back, despite what he would hear—and he would hear plenty."[16]

So on August 28, 1945, Branch Rickey and Jackie Robinson met at the Brooklyn Dodgers' headquarters in New York City. It would be a meeting that would not only change each man's life but would arouse the moral conscience of a nation. During the meeting Rickey explained how he wanted Robinson to play for their minor league team in Montreal and then the Brooklyn Dodgers. This would effectively make Jackie Robinson the first African American to play Major League baseball in the modern era. Rickey explained that if Robinson would agree to this, he would endure mistreatment of the worse kind. He would be exposed to vulgar and violent racist slurs and could never retaliate. Rickey appealed to the common faith the two men shared and handed him a copy of a book titled *Life of Christ* by Giovanni Papini. He referenced Matthew 5:39, where Jesus said, "If anyone slaps you on the right cheek, turn to him the other also." Robinson felt with God's strength he could accomplish this task.

> So Jackie Roosevelt Robinson and Branch Rickey shook hands. And there, in that fourth-floor office in Brooklyn to which Jackie had ridden in a whites-only elevator, under a portrait of Abraham Lincoln, history was made. It was a momentous day not only for baseball but for America.[17]

In the years that followed, Robinson kept his word and was a steady portrait of someone who had the guts not to fight back. He was and is one of the greatest examples of patient diligence, of a dreamer who would not be moved to violence or verbal outbursts. He stayed the course, and through his conviction-fueled endurance, the dream of integration in baseball became a reality.

The dreamer of the day has to endure. He or she must have the grit and determination to stay the course. An undeterred dreamer can change the world, especially when the endurance finds its power, as Jackie Robinson did, in the gospel.

CELEBRATE VICTORIES, BUT REST ONLY WHEN THE DREAM IS REALIZED

I have already written about William Wilberforce, but such a leader and such a life can illuminate our thinking on multiple levels. Wilberforce dreamed of a day when his country would no longer be involved with the slave trade and when all living under a British flag would be free. The first major victory occurred when the bill for the Slave Trade Act was carried by a majority vote in early 1807, making abolition a government measure. Following the introduction of the bill and before the second reading, fellow abolitionist Sir Samuel Romilly was giving a speech in which he was complimenting and giving tribute to Wilberforce's tireless efforts. At one point he stated,

When he retires into the bosom of his happy and delighted family, when he lays himself down on his bed, reflecting on the innumerable voices that will be raised in every quarter of the world to bless him, how much more pure and perfect felicity must he enjoy, in the consciousness of having preserved so many millions of his fellow-creatures.[18]

At this point in the speech several rounds of cheering broke out all through the House. Overcome with emotion from the twenty-year fight for abolition, Wilberforce sat with his head in his hands and tears streaming down his face.

There was still another victory to be had before Wilberforce's dream could be realized. The selling and buying of slaves was no longer legal, but the practice of slavery continued with nearly one million people being treated as property under the British flag. The efforts toward the emancipation of all slaves in the British Empire would consume Wilberforce's efforts for the next almost thirty years. In June of 1833, a seventy-three-year-old William Wilberforce, who was in failing health, made his way back to London to see a trusted doctor.

While in London he stayed with his cousin Lucy Smith at 44 Cadogan Place, near Sloane Street. Hague summarized his return to London as "at least on the part of others—in no way in anticipation of his approaching death, but as it happened it reunited him for the final ten days of his life with the people and events of the political world among whom he had felt at home for so long."[19] During this time the final push toward complete abolition and emancipation was winding down. On Friday, July 26, he felt well enough to be carried in a chair outside to enjoy the fresh air. His youngest son, Henry, was with him at this time and observed of his father sitting outside, "He presented a most striking appearance, looking forth with calm delight upon trees and grass, the freshness and vigour of which contrasted with his own decay."[20] This was the last time Wilberforce would view God's creation before his passing. That night the Bill for the Abolition of Slavery was read for the second time in the House, and the last public news Wilberforce received in his lifetime was that the cause of his life at last enjoyed a successful conclusion. He responded, "Thank God that I should have lived to witness a day in which England is willing to give twenty millions sterling for the Abolition of Slavery."[21]

Within twenty-four hours, his health began a steep decline again, and by that Sunday night he was fainting and losing his memory. But before he died, he could rest knowing that by August 1834, the eight hundred thousand slaves living in different colonies across the British Empire would be free. Hague summarized, "And so, with extraordinary poignancy and symmetry, the man who had labored for nearly fifty years to promote measures that would one day lead to the emancipation of the slaves knew, at the very end of the seventy-three years and eleven months of his life, that this goal had been accomplished."[22]

Wilberforce is a great example of someone who exhausted himself for a cause. There is a stubborn tenacity that must exist within you if you are going to see your dream through to completion. Along the way, you must celebrate the victories, small and big, while allowing yourself to be motivated by the ultimate realization of the dream. Until the dream comes to fruition, there is still plenty of work to be done.

———

I know all this may seem a little extreme, but dreamers are not striving for balance any more than an artist is motivated by a business plan. You see, dreamers, like artists, are motivated by passion. To quote a line I heard from a recent commencement speech given by actor Robert De Niro, "When it comes to the arts, passion should always trump common sense." I think all dreamers should be so passionate about their dream they do not wait for the permission that comes from common-sense type thinking. Rather, they should move forward boldly and passionately, pursuing the impossible as if someone's life depended upon it . . . because many times it does. And they shouldn't rest until at last their dream has come to pass.

7 DAYS, 7 PASSPORTS, 7 QUESTIONS

Life goes by so fast, doesn't it? I am writing this chapter at thirty thousand feet somewhere between Toronto and Orlando. It is amazing that in just a couple of hours I can go from one city in one country to my home city in another country. Life, more and more to me, seems like a quick trip. You take off, you land, and you have some time to redeem in between. I do not have any control about when we pull back from the gate in Toronto or when the wheels will touch down on the runway in Orlando, but I have a lot of say about the moments in between.

I had to get a passport stamped upon entering Canada and upon returning to the United States. I travel quite a bit and have been to countries all over the world. My passport is stamped on every page, ragged around the edges, and generally looks like it went through the washing machine. I made my first overseas trip when I was sixteen years old, at which time I went through the process of acquiring a passport. A passport, once issued, is good for ten years, and then you need a new one. In my life I will only have seven passports. That is a handful of pages in each passport littered with stamps. This can be a bit depressing, causing me to wonder about the delicacy and frailness of life. Or I can simply look at the situation and decide that my seven passports will be full of intentionality, with each stamp telling another story in the adventure of following Jesus.

In the end, all of life can shrink down into seven days, seven passports, and also seven decisions. The beautiful thing about life is that God delights in and blesses this kind of approach. He wants us to influence, use our time well, live with a sense of calling, engage a broken world, build healthy relationships, be rightly motivated, and dream about the seemingly impossible. So based on all that we have studied over the seven-day template, I want to leave you with seven questions:

1. How will you utilize the influence that God gives you and allows you to develop?

2. How will you redeem the time you have been given and manage it in such a way that you tell a type of story others will want to emulate?

3. How can you read God into the everyday part of your life: family, work, being a member of society, and a part of the movement of Christianity?

4. How will you engage in your culture, or someone else's, as an agent of redemption, seeking to preserve and illuminate it for the cause of Christ?

5. What types of friendships and community will you seek out so your soul can be cared for and you can care for others?

6. How will you pursue the invisible labor of being rightly motivated?

7. How do you answer the question, "What would I do for the glory of God if I knew I would not fail?"

Life is a lot like taking off and landing; it is a series of passports that are issued and reissued. We did not choose when or where we were born and we do not control when we will punch out, but there is a lot we can do about the moments in between. We decide how our pages will be filled. And oh, how important those decisions and moments are!

As we have already seen C. S. Lewis describe, the moments of life are our title page for eternity. Or rather, life is just the introduction to the greater story that will never end. But while we're on this earth, never stop in your quest to make all the moments of life matter with a sacred sense of intentionality . . . yes, with a sacred intent.

SACRED INTENT REFLECTIONS AND PRAYERS

Now that you've finished reading *Sacred Intent*, this appendix is an opportunity for you to meditate on the book's principles and allow them to permeate your life. Focus on one area every day of the week, reading reflections from each section and using the prayer to guide you.

MONDAY: INFLUENCE

- I give myself permission to start anew, and there's no better day than today to start something or to start believing something about myself.

- Thanks to an independent mind-set coupled with initiative and a desire to accomplish something measurable, I know that I matter and can make a difference today.

- I was created in the image of God, and as a human being I am the crown of God's creation. I know I'm created to influence.

- I'm a steward of God's creation, so his name should echo through my influence wherever I am—whether at home, in my community, or on the other side of the world.

- Living my life at the feet of Jesus is where my leadership finds its meaning and motivation.

- I will have a lasting effect in this world because I'm a coconspirator with God, and he will not and cannot fail.

- Joshua's leadership experiences were book-ended by Moses' prayers, so I will begin and end each day in prayer.

- I will have a richer and fuller life as I pray, obey, and celebrate, completely trusting God to bless me with victory and success for his glory.

- I will choose mentors who are good examples for me to follow, as well as strive to be someone others can follow.

- I will not have a spirit of fear (focusing on self) but a spirit of power, love, and self-control that helps me focus on Jesus and have a *Christocentric* attitude.

- I will guard truth so a rich heritage of right belief is passed down from my generation to the next.

- With the knowledge that I will one day see Jesus face to face, coupled with the inspiration of the Holy Spirit, God has given me a crystal-clear roadmap to leadership.

God, thank you for the sun coming up this morning, which reminds me of your mercy toward mankind and, more personally, of your mercy and grace in my life. And so, as the sunlight touches the landscape of your creation it demonstrates your authority and my responsibility as the crown of your creation. You have created me to exercise influence within your creation. Therefore I commit to use the influence you have given me to contribute toward your desires, O Lord, for your creation.

Jesus, I ask you for a mentor that embodies the same characteristics of great mentors in the Scriptures, like Moses and Paul. May he or she be a source of encouragement, pointing me to a Christ-centered attitude, unashamed of your gospel, teaching me to always protect the truth, as I pursue godly living. May you send a mentor who will guide me to understand the impact of the Scriptures and how I am part of your mission.

I ask these things of you, O God, because I wish to serve you well with the moments that I have been given. Please guard my heart from the desire of fame and the inclination for my name to be known. May any influence I have lift high the name and fame of Jesus. Amen.

TUESDAY: TIME

- How I use my time is a reflection of my understanding (or misunderstanding) of God's purpose for my life, so I will be intentional with every minute and every hour.

- I will care deeply about the gift of time because my life is part of a much larger story known as history.

- All my daily tasks, events, and decisions make up my story, so I control what will one day be seen as the central theme of my life.

- Through time management, I will saturate all my activities with divine purpose by making sure they are consistent with each season God gives me.

- By understanding the blessing of the moment, I am reminded of God's mercy.

- Time management is more about capturing the moments of life as an act of worship than about managing them.

- It is my spiritual responsibility to own my schedule instead of letting it own me.

- Through a spirit of intentionality, I will keep focused on God and the work of the Holy Spirit in me.

- I will view my life through the eyes of a movie producer so I can remain focused on the heart of my story at all times.

- Who I spend my time with is one of the most important decisions I make, because it determines who are the main characters in my story.

- Benjamin Franklin said, "If you fail to plan, you are planning to fail!" So I will do all I can to find what time-management tool works best for me.

- Past failures will not defeat me, but they'll motivate me as I move forward and strive to never waste time again.

God, I begin by recognizing that time is a gift and thus a demonstration of your grace. I am also conscious that even though time appears so infinite to me, it really is like a vapor or a wisp of fog that vanishes before my very eyes. I commit to be purposeful with the moments you have granted me. God, I commit to use the time given me to accomplish all the tasks you have for me. And in so doing my desire, my commitment, is that I constantly focus on living out a story with your redemption as its central theme.

For any time I have wasted I ask your forgiveness. I commit that this day my life will be a living sacrifice experiencing each moment as if it were my last opportunity to be obedient to your desired will for my life. I will manage my time so that I live with purpose because I live on purpose. Amen.

WEDNESDAY: CALLING

- Instead of seeing my calling as a matter of what *I* should do, I will focus on what *God* does in and through whatever I do.

- Salvation cannot be earned but is received only by grace through faith, and the Bible is God's divine source for revealed knowledge.

- I am called by God an everyday priest, chosen to carry out his great cause of advancing the name of Jesus and the church.

- Regardless of my vocation—graphic designer, third-grade teacher, butcher, baker, or candlestick maker—my true calling is to make sure God is obvious in my work as I contribute to society.

- While reading God into daily work defines a standard of excellence, determination, and a right attitude, I know that he is most obvious simply in my motivations.

- Because God's calling is influenced through church, family, citizenship, and contributions to society, I will not elevate one element of my calling above another.

- When someone asks me, "What do you do?" I will be ready with a response that really answers "Who are you?"

- Instead of trying to run faster, harder, and accomplish more, I will keep my eyes on Jesus in all things and at all times so I'm actually burdened less in my life's "race."

- I will give Jesus all of my burdens, which I was never intended to shoulder alone.

- The best I can ever accomplish on my own is nothing more than "refrigerator art"—so I will trust God to create a masterpiece through my life.

- I am a co-laborer with the King, yoked with Jesus by grace and love, so my calling is not about *doing more* but *living more* through Christ.

- My calling is all about pursuing the identity God provides for me as opposed to trying to create my own sense of identity through family, career, or any role I play.

God, I recognize that I have been blessed to live a life rich with calling. And so I say thank you for pulling me out of darkness and into the marvelous light of following Jesus and to be a part of his Church. Thank you for my family. Thank you for allowing me to be a part of a culture, or rather a citizen in a nation, that protects me and affords me certain freedoms. Thank you for the talents you have given me and allowing me to cultivate them in such a way that they could become my vocation. The multiplicity of callings you have placed on my life is a constant reminder of your grace in my life. Every time I look in the mirror, go to church, see my family, walk the streets of my city, or go to work, I am reminded of your goodness. Lord, I commit to live ever aware that my life is saturated with calling; thus I will live a life full of sacred intent. Amen.

THURSDAY: ENGAGEMENT

- Because I am blessed by God, I will live out that blessing by being salt *and* light to the world around me.

- I will live a life that is stamped with purpose, daily committed to what matters most.

- Because I have placed my faith in Christ Jesus and have begun to grasp the grandness of God's story, I will help the hopeless hold on until hope arrives.

- I am not called to be "sugary sweet" (giving false hope) or "spicy hot" (always confrontational), but to be salt that preserves the gospel.

- Jesus is the light of the world—without an on/off switch—illuminating the darkest corners and the farthest reaches of this world.

- As a follower of Christ, I do not walk in darkness but have the light of life, so my influence and engagement should never be limited and always be brave and courageous.

- As salt and light in Christ, when I engage with others, may they experience God because they have seen a little bit of heaven in me.

- I will remember and learn from the community of men and women who would not relent until they had transformed the world around them.

- Following William Wilberforce's example, I will align myself with my own group of spiritual allies with whom to converse, strategize, and pray for reform.

- I will strive to always keep Jesus at the center of my friendships and communities so justice is valued throughout the world.

- I will stand up for those being bullied, care for those being victimized, and bring relief to those who have lost homes and even family members all in the name of Jesus.

- I am devoted to changing my world so that it determines where I live, whom I'm intimately connected with, and how I spend my leisure time.

God, I am a pilgrim making my journey home to the celestial city that is heaven. So today I realize that a significant part of that journey is engaging the culture in which you have placed me. Because of your blessing that flowed downward from heaven, I know I was a spiritually dead corpse before you gave me life and purpose. Because I have seen the unseen in you, Jesus—the image of the invisible God—and because I have begun to grasp the purpose of your story, I realize my role as an element of preservation and protection for a morally corrupt and spiritually blind world. I ask you to help me to be salt, to preserve and protect, with both grace and truth. I also ask that you help me to illuminate those around me to the hope and purpose that can only be found in you. And I pray to this end, that people would observe my life being salt and light, and that they would worship you, O God in heaven. Amen.

FRIDAY: RELATIONSHIPS

- My relationships are of utmost importance, since the type of relationships I build will determine the capacity to imagine, collaborate, and discover.

- With the right relationships I can become a better version of myself and help others become better versions of themselves.

- Sometimes I must sacrifice my comfort or even freedom to take care of a "comrade" who, above anything else, must be taken care of first.

- Accountability happens among my closest friends as we care for each other's souls and help one another be rooted and built up in Jesus and established in the faith.

- For real, healthy, life-giving relationships to exist, at times I must fulfill the role of doctor (giving help) while other times I must humbly be the patient (receiving care from others).

- My friendships will revolve around an "if you go, we go" type of attitude—we will have each other's back no matter what.

- I will not allow my inner circle of friends to just sit around and look at *each other*. I want my inner circle of friends to surround *King Jesus* and focus on his desires and commands.

- I can accomplish more by collaborating with others than I could eve do on my own—as Dr. Jay Strack says, "All of us are smarter than any one of us."

- Because the disciples collaborated with God's great rescue plan for humanity, Christ followers throughout history have continued to do the same—and I will do no different.

- I want my life to matter, to be alive with purpose, and to make this world better, and there's no better way to accomplish more—maybe even something extraordinary!—than by collaborating with others.

- Ideas are never just ideas but the foundations on which I can build my actions and, ultimately, my life.

- I must have a collaborative mindset at all times, because . . . *We > Me!*

God, thank you for the gift of relationship. I am so grateful for friends and loved ones and could spend hours expressing my gratitude for each relationship and the role it has in my life. Today I commit to care for my friends and loved ones and to make myself available to their care as well. Help me to love those around me as I love my own soul, demonstrating such qualities of friendship as love, oneness, loyalty, counsel, kindness, honesty, sacrifice, obedience, communication, self-control, and character.

Lord, please help me to never fall into the trap of seeing myself as a maverick, where victory or defeat rests squarely on my shoulders. But let me pursue life's tasks with cohorts, with each of us sharing the weight of responsibility. Jesus, thank you for demonstrating teamwork with your disciples and providing such an amazing example to follow. I ask, oh God, for your favor as I build friendships and relationships so that together we accomplish exponentially more for the name of Jesus. Amen.

SATURDAY: MOTIVATIONS

- Because of what Christ has done in my life through salvation, I can kill off my old, sinful ways and live a triumphant life.

- A life that is rightly motivated is rightly focused . . . and a life rightly focused is full of obedience . . . and a life of obedience finishes the adventure fully confident and approved by our heavenly Father.

- To live a life full of sacred intent involves me doing battle with the "old man" or "the flesh" on a daily basis—knowing that I am more than a conqueror in Christ.

- I am a giant killer in Christ, and, like David, I will be prepared, be quick to act, and will aim to kill the enemy within.

- I will work at being *the next humblest version of me,* as Bob Goff puts it, striving to have a healthy prayer life, live a life mindful of grace, and consider others first.

- I will flee from sexual immorality (in any and all forms)—not just running away from it but racing toward Jesus.

- I want to live with a sacred intent and experience all that God has for me, which is so much more than the hashtags, 140-character messages, and double-taps I usually focus on.

- Since every adventure has a beginning, then I want the genesis of mine to come from a concern for the movement of Christianity and the global church.

- The story of my life is woven together with millions of stories from Christians across the world and throughout time to create something much greater—the story of God's people.

- God's story is told in four parts: 1) His perfect creation; 2) mankind's rebellion; 3) redemption through Jesus; and 4) God's restoration, making all things new again.

- The bigger story of which I am a part cannot be contained and has no borders, for the supernatural doesn't fit in boxes made by human hands.

- Through adventure I will discover, or rediscover, my identity. Jesus was and is central to the mission of God, and to be called to a relationship with Jesus is to be called to the adventure that is his mission.

God, on this day I humbly approach you concerning the motivations of my life. It seems that at any given time, with any given event, I find it hard to have a completely God-honoring intent. And so it is on this day that I ask you to purge from me any false or unhealthy motivations that represent the old man. May the disease of me that is pride be destroyed . . . may I flee from any hint of sexual immorality . . . may I have singularity in attention to the goal and prize that is Jesus . . . may I fight the flesh at every turn . . . and may my understanding of success forever find its meaning in the phrase obedience to the faith. I long that the adventure of following you, Jesus, be so all-consuming that it saturates every motivating factor of my life. I commit that my life be an adventure that continually pursues your mission, God, and that through this great journey I discover—and rediscover again and again—the identity you have given me in Christ Jesus. Amen.

SUNDAY: DREAMING

- I will not be satisfied with dreaming at night of things I cannot remember—I want to dream during the day of ideas that can turn the world upside down.

- Today is a great day to imagine the impossible, to focus on the conviction and strategy necessary to change the world for the glory of God.

- Every dream of mine must begin by answering this question: "What would I do with my life if I knew I would not fail?"

- A great dream always envisions some sort of change in this world—but before I have a dream, I need conviction and to be firmly rooted, being built up, and walking in Christ Jesus.

- When I think of past dreamers, I will recognize greatness and opportunity rather than just a wonderful story.

- Dreaming is not reserved for those who fit a certain image—it is for all who have been made in the image of God.

- A dreamer must cast vision in such a way that others understand and feel the sense of urgency and need.

- I may conceive the dream, but any dream will always be bigger than one person.

- Think big but start small. I must implement and pursue my dream at a micro level so it can ultimately be effective at a macro level.

- To change the world, I need allies to rally around my dream—and the strongest team may be one that nobody else would ever have thought to assemble.

- Dreams that change the world are often a slow burn, illuminating the possibility of what could be.

- I am so passionate about my dream that I will not wait for permission from common-sense-type thinking. I will move forward boldly, pursuing the impossible as if someone's life depends upon it.

God, thank you for the resurrection of Jesus from the dead. The empty tomb is a daily reminder that all things are possible with God. And so I bring to you my dream, the answer to the question, "What would I do for the glory of God if I knew I would not fail?" You have given me the gift of imagination, and I am seeking to exercise that gift to change the world in such a way that is consistent with your desired will as expressed in Scripture. If this dream is from you, please bring it to fruition.

Lord, help my focus to remain on you, even as others look at me and focus on appearances, age, or the odds of my dream coming true. Give me favor to cast vision in a compelling manner and surround me with fellow dreamers who fully believe in what you have placed in my heart. Give me strength when the days are long and fatigue sets in. Grant me patience and determination that can only come from you. In everything I give you thanks, praying the words of Ephesians 3:20–21: "Now to him who is able to do far more abundantly than all that we ask or think, according to the power at work within us, to him be glory in the church and in Christ Jesus throughout all generations, forever and ever. Amen."

NOTES

Prologue

1. J. B. Polhill, *Acts,* vol. 26 of *The New American Commentary* (Nashville: Broadman & Holman Publishers, 1992), 95.

Monday

1. See the discussion of Genesis theme in Gleason Archer, *A Survey Of Old Testament* (Chicago: Moody, 1996), 179–219.
2. Summarized from: Robert Jamieson, A. R. Fausset, and David Brown, "Genesis 1:26," *Commentary Critical and Explanatory on the Whole Bible* (Oak Harbor, WA: Logos Research Systems, Inc., 1997).
3. Brent Crowe, *Chasing Elephants* (Colorado Springs: NavPress, 2010), 13.
4. Edghar H. Schein, *Organizational Culture and Leadership* (Indianapolis: Jossey-Bass, 2010), 3.
5. Bill Bright, *God: Discover His Character* (Nottingham: New Life Publishing, 1999), 86.
6. Oswald Chambers, *My Utmost for His Highest* (Grand Rapids, MI: Discovery House Publishers, 1992), June 19 entry.
7. J. Oswald Sanders, *Spiritual Leadership* (Chicago: Moody Publishers, 2007), 27.
8. Christopher J. H. Wright, *The Mission of God* (Downers Grove: IVP Academic Press, 2006), 23.
9. C. F. Keil and F. Delitzsch, *Commentary on the Old Testament: Pentateuch* (Peabody: Hendrickson, 2001), 371.
10. Ronald E. Clements, *The Cambridge Bible Commentary: Exodus* (New York: Cambridge University Press, 1972), 103.
11. Keil and Delitzsch, *Commentary on the Old Testament: Pentateuch,* 372.
12. Ibid.
13. John Calvin, *Calvin's Commentaries: Harmony of Exodus, Leviticus, Numbers, Deuteronomy,* Vol. II (Grand Rapids: Baker Books, 2005), 294.
14. Ibid., 294–95.
15. Keil and Delitzsch, *Commentary on the Old Testament: Pentateuch,* 468.
16. R. Laird Harris, Gleason L. Archer, Jr., and Bruce Waltke, *Theological Wordbook of the Old Testament* (Chicago: Moody Publishers; New Edition), 958.
17. Keil and Delitzsch, *Commentary on the Old Testament: Pentateuch,* 465.
18. Calvin, *Calvin's Commentaries: Harmony of Exodus, Leviticus, Numbers, Deuteronomy* (Vol. III), 369.
19. Tomas D. Lea and Hayne P. Griffin, *1, 2 Timothy, Titus,* vol. 34 from *The New American Commentary Series* (electronic Logos Library System), (Nashville: Broadman & Holman Publishers, 2001), 182–183.
20. Richard C. H. Lenski, "Interpretation of Second Timothy," vol. 9 *(Colossians, 1–2 Thessalonians, 1–2 Timothy, Titus, Philemon)* of *Commentary on the New Testament* (Peabody: Hendrickson, 2001), 742.

21. Andreas Köstenberger, "2 Timothy," vol. 12 *(Ephesians-Philemon)* of *The Expositor's Bible Commentary* (Grand Rapids: Zondervan, 2006), 568.

22. Ibid.

23. Lenski, "Interpretation of Second Timothy," 749.

24. Köstenberger, "2 Timothy," 568.

25. Spiros Zodhiates, *The Complete Word Study Dictionary: New Testament* (Chattanooga, TN: AMG Publishers, 2000), electronic edition.

26. Lea and Griffin, *1, 2 Timothy, Titus,* 189.

27. Ibid., 190.

28. Andrew Robert Fausset, Robert Jamieson, and David Brown, "2 Timothy 1:7," *A Commentary, Critical and Explanatory, on the Whole Bible* (Oak Harbor, WA: Logos Research Systems, Inc., 1997), electronic edition.

29. J. Oswald Sanders, *Spiritual Leadership* (Chicago: Moody Publishers, 2007), 118.

30. Sanders, *Spiritual Leadership,* 118–19.

31. J. Swanson, "Greek," *Dictionary of Biblical Languages with Semantic Domains (New Testament),* (Oak Harbor: Logos Research Systems, Inc., 1997), electronic edition.

32. Köstenberger, "2 Timothy," 584.

33. Ibid.

34. Marvin Richardson Vincent, "2 Timothy 3:16," *Word Studies in the New Testament* (Bellingham: Logos Research Systems, Inc., 2002), electronic edition.

35. J. Swanson, "Greek," electronic edition.

36. William Barclay, *The Letters to Timothy, Titus, and Philemon* in *The Daily Study Bible Series,* Rev. ed. (Philadelphia: The Westminster Press, 2000), electronic edition.

37. Lea and Griffin, *1, 2 Timothy, Titus,* 237.

38. R. C. H. Lenski, "Interpretation of Second Timothy," 847.

39. Andreas Köstenberger, "2 Timothy," 591.

Tuesday

1. Christopher Marlowe, *Doctor Faustus* (New York: New American Library: 1969, c. 2001), 93.

2. Ibid., 15.

3. Ibid., 80–81.

4. Dietrich Bonhoeffer, *Discipleship*: *Dietrich Bonhoeffer Works 4* (Minneapolis: Fortress Press, 2003), 43.

5. Ibid., 45.

6. See definition at http://www.merriam-webster.com/dictionary/time.

7. For explanation of this phrase, go to http://dictionary.reference.com/browse/knee-high+to+a+grasshopper.

8. Wayne Grudem, *Systematic Theology* (Grand Rapids: Zondervan, 1994), 169.

9. Wayne Martindale and Jerry Root, eds., *The Quotable Lewis* (Carol Stream: Tyndale House, 1990), 581.

10. C. S. Lewis, *The Last Battle* (New York: Harper Collins: 1956), 228.

11. The phrase "the soul's autobiography" appears in Henrietta Mears, *What The Bible Is All About,* (Ventura: Regal Books: 1983), 201.

12. D. A. Carson, R. T. France, J. A. Motyer and G. J. Wenham, eds., *New Bible commentary: 21st century edition*, 4th ed. (Downers Grove: Inter-Varsity Press, 1994), 612.

13. Toby Keith, "Should've Been a Cowboy," *Toby Keith* (Mercury Records/PolyGram, 1993).

14. S. Zodhiates, *The Complete Word Study Dictionary: New Testament*, electronic ed.

15. John Calvin, *Commentaries on the Epistle of Paul the Apostle to the Romans* (Edinburgh: The Calvin Translation Society, 1849), 452.

16. Marvin Richardson Vincent, "Romans 12:1," *Word Studies in the New Testament* (New York: Charles Scribner's Sons, 1887).

17. John Chrysostom, "Homilies of St. John Chrysostom, Archbishop of Constantinople, on the Epistle of St. Paul to the Romans" (translated by J. B. Morris, W. H. Simcox & G. B. Stevens), *Saint Chrysostom: Homilies on the Acts of the Apostles and the Epistle to the Romans*, vol. 11 of *A Select Library of the Nicene and Post-Nicene Fathers of the Christian Church, First Series* (New York: Christian Literature Company, 1889), 496.

18. Kenneth Samuel Wuest, "Romans 12:1," *Wuest's Word Studies from the Greek New Testament for the English Reader* (Grand Rapids: Eerdmans, 1997).

19. Wuest, "Ephesians 5:15," *Wuest's Word Studies from the Greek New Testament for the English Reader*.

20. Chuck Swindoll, *Strengthening Your Grip* (Nashville: Worthy Publishing, 2015), 227.

21. Lea and Griffin, *1, 2 Timothy, Titus,* 189.

22. Theodore B. Backer, *A Compact Anthology of Bartlett's Quotation's* (Middle Village, NY: Jonathan David Publishers, 1974), 53.

23. Since then retitled: Andy Stanley, *When Work and Family Collide: Keeping Your Job from Cheating Your Family* (Colorado Springs: Multnomah Books, 2011).

24. Much of this section was inspired by the sermon "Choosing to Cheat" by Andy Stanley; http://northpoint.org/messages/breathing-room/choosing-to-cheat

25. *William Wilberforce: A Hero for Humanity* is the title of Kevin Belmonte's biography of Wilberforce.

26. Samuel Wilberforce and Robert Wilberforce, *The Life of William Wilberforce* (Philadelphia: Henry Perkins, 1839), 16.

27. Ibid.

28. Robin Furneaux, *William Wilberforce*, (Vancouver: Regent College Publishing, 2006), 11.

29. Kevin Belmonte, *William Wilberforce: Hero for Humanity*, (Grand Rapids: Zondervan, 2007), 45.

30. John Pollock, *Wilberforce* (London: Constable and Company, 1977), 7.

31. Sylvanus Urban, "Obituary: William Wilberforce, Esq.," *The Gentleman's Magazine and Historical Chronicle,* Issue 103, Part 2 (London: J. B. Nichols and Son, 1833), 273.

32. Pollock, *Wilberforce,* 7.

33. Wilberforce and Wilberforce, *The Life of William Wilberforce,* 17.

34. Ibid.

Wednesday

1. Mark Galli and Ted Olsen, *131 Christians Everyone Should Know* (Nashville: Broadman & Holman, 2000), 33.

2. See http://www.merriam-webster.com/dictionary/indulgence.

3. Gene Edward Veith, *God at Work* (Wheaton: Crossway Books, 2001), 17.

4. Veith, *God at Work*, 24.

5. Veith, *God at Work*, 48.

6. Herbert Lockyer, ed., *Nelson's Illustrated Bible Dictionary* (Nashville: Thomas Nelson, 1986), 1030–31.

7. M. Easton, *Easton's Bible Dictionary* (Oak Harbor: Logos Research Systems, 1996).

8. John Calvin, *John 12–21, Acts 1–13,* vol. XVIII of *Calvin's Commentary* (Grand Rapids: Baker, 2005), 366.

9. R. C. H. Lenski, "Acts," *Commentary on the New Testament* (Peabody: Hendrickson, 2001), 353.

10. John B. Polhill, "Acts 9:16" from vol. 26 of *The New American Commentary* (Nashville: Broadman & Holman Publishers, 2001).

11. Lenski, "Acts," 363.

12. Robert Jamieson, Andrew R. Fausset, and David Brown, "Acts 9:15," *A Commentary, Critical and Explanatory, on the Old and New Testaments,* (Oak Harbor: Logos Research Systems, Inc., 1997).

13. Polhill, "Acts 9:16."

14. Os Guinness, *The Call* (Nashville: Word Publishing, 1998), 4.

15. R. K. Harrison, ed., *Encyclopedia of Biblical and Christian Ethics* (Nashville: Thomas Nelson, 1987), 247.

16. Tokumnboh Adeyemo, ed, *African Bible Commentary* (Nairobi, Kenya: Word Publishers, 2006), 112.

17. Veith, *God at Work*, 96.

18. C. S. Lewis, *The Chronicles of Narnia* (New York: HarperCollins, 1982), 83.

19. Walter A. Elwell, and Philip W. Comfort, eds., *Tyndale Bible Dictionary (Tyndale Reference Library),* (Wheaton, IL: Tyndale House Publishers, 2001), 1318–1319.

20. A. Robertson, "Matthew 11:29," *Word Pictures in the New Testament* (Nashville: Broadman Press, 1933).

Thursday

1. John Stott, *Involvement* (Old Tappan, NJ: Fleming H. Revell Company 1985), 19.

2. Ibid., 35.

3. "The song of God's justice" is a phrase that appears in John Calvin's *Golden Booklet of the True Christian Life* (Grand Rapids: Baker Books, 1952), 11.

4. Alvin Schmidt, *How Christianity Changed the World*, (Grand Rapids: Zondervan, 2004), 16.

5. James M. Freeman, and Harold J. Chadwick, *Manners & Customs of the Bible* (North Brunswick: Bridge-Logos Publishers, 1998), 143.

6. R. B. Hughes and J. C. Laney, *Tyndale Concise Bible Commentary (The Tyndale Reference Library),* (Wheaton: Tyndale House Publishers, 2001), 433.

7. M. S. Mills, "Matthew 5:13," *The Life of Christ: A Study Guide to the Gospel Record* (Dallas: 3E Ministries, 1999).

8. See http://passioncitychurch.com/watch/message/QaRA_yB7u3tr

NOTES

9. William Barclay, ed., *The Gospel of Matthew,* vol. 1 from *The Daily Study Bible Series* (Philadelphia: The Westminster John Knox Press, 1976).

10. Bob Goff, *Love Does* (Nashville: Thomas Nelson, 2012), 31.

11. See Leon Morris's discussion on "light" in *The Gospel According to Matthew* (Grand Rapids: Eerdmans Publishing Company, 1992), 104–105.

12. John Wolffe, "Wilberforce, William (1759–1833)," (Oxford: *Oxford Dictionary of National Biography* first published 2004; online ed, May 2009), http://www.oxforddnb.com/view/article/29386

13. William Hague, *William Wilberforce* (London: HarperCollins Publishers, 2007), 218.

14. Ibid., 219.

15. Ibid., 220.

16. See Hague, *William Wilberforce,* 220–221, for a list of reforms made by the Clapham Sect in the twelve years following 1792.

17. John Piper, *Amazing Grace in the Life of William Wilberforce* (Wheaton: Crossway Books, 2006), 55.

18. Os Guinness, *Character Counts* (Grand Rapids: Baker Books, 1999), 88.

19. Wilberforce and Wilberforce, *The Life of William Wilberforce,* 170.

20. Hague, *William Wilberforce,* 220–221.

21. Wilberforce and Wilberforce, *The Life of William Wilberforce,* 82.

Friday

1. Viktor E. Frankl, *Man's Search for Meaning.* (Boston: Beacon Press, 2006), 58–59.

2. Jamieson, Fausset, and Brown, "1 Samuel 18:4," *A Commentary, Critical and Explanatory, on the Old and New Testaments.*

3. C. S. Lewis, *The Quotable Lewis* (Wheaton: Tyndale House Publishers, 1990), 237.

4. Matthew Henry, "Proverbs 18:24," *Matthew Henry's Commentary on the Whole Bible: Complete and Unabridged in One Volume* (Peabody: Hendrickson, 1996, c 1991).

5. Paul L. Tan, *Encyclopedia of 7700 illustrations: A treasury of illustrations, anecdotes, facts and quotations for pastors, teachers and Christian workers* (Garland: Bible Communications, 1996, c1979).

6. For an online definition of this term, go to http://dictionary.reference.com/browse/fair-weather+friend

7. Tan, *Encyclopedia of 7700 illustrations: A treasury of illustrations, anecdotes, facts and quotations for pastors, teachers and Christian workers.*

8. Warren W. Wiersbe, "John 15:12," *The Bible Exposition Commentary* (Wheaton: Victor Books, 1996, c1989).

9. John Phillips, *Exploring Proverbs, Vol. 1 (The John Phillips Commentary Series),* (Grand Rapids: Kregel Publications, 1996), 415.

10. James Kouzes and Barry Posner, *The Leadership Challenge* (San Francisco: John Wiley and Sons, 2007), 218–274.

11. Kouzes and Posner, *The Leadership Challenge,* 223.

12. Today Wroclaw in Poland.

13. Eric Metaxas, *Seven Men: And the Secret of their Greatness* (Nashville: Thomas Nelson Publishers, 2013), 92.

14. Dietrich Bonhoeffer, *Berlin: 1932–1933*. Introduction by L. L. Rasmussen, ed., to the English edition (DBW 12; ed. I. Best, D. Higgins and D. W. Stott; translated by C. Nicolaisen and E. Scharffenorth), (Minneapolis: Fortress Press 2009), 3.

15. See http://www.kz-gedenkstaette-dachau.de/index-e.html, accessed October 20, 2013.

16. Geffrey Kelly and F. Burton Nelson, eds., *Testament of Freedom* (New York: Harper Collins, 1995), 532.

17. Summarized from John Toland, *Hitler* (Hertfordshire: Wordsworth Editions Limited, 1997), 329–358.

18. Ibid., 358.

19. Ibid., 319.

20. Kelly and Nelson, eds., *Testament of Freedom,* 36.

21. Eberhard Bethge, *Dietrich Bonhoeffer: A Biography* (Minneapolis: Fortress Press, 2000), 623.

22. Ibid., 672.

23. Ibid., 936.

24. Renate Bethge and Christian Gremmels, eds., *Dietrich Bonhoeffer: A Life in Pictures* (Minneapolis: Fortress Press, 2006), 150.

25. That fact that Bonhoeffer was part of the inner circle of the conspiracy in the Abwehr is further confirmed by Renate Bethge in *Dietrich Bonhoeffer: A Life in Pictures*, 124.

26. Eric Metaxas, *Bonhoeffer: Pastor, Martyr, Prophet, Spy* (Nashville: Thomas Nelson Publishers, 2010), 320.

27. Dietrich Bonhoeffer, *Conspiracy and Imprisonment: 1940–1945* (Minneapolis: Fortress Press, 2006), 701.

28. Ibid.

29. Kelly and Nelson, eds., *A Testament to Freedom,* 42.

30. Ibid., 42–43.

31. Bonhoeffer, *Conspiracy and Imprisonment: 1940–1945,* 702.

32. Ibid.

33. Summarized from Bethge's, *Dietrich Bonhoeffer,* "Chronology," 1027.

34. Ibid., 928.

35. Wolf-Dieter Zimmermann and Ronald Gregor Smith eds., *I Knew Dietrich Bonhoeffer* (New York: Harper and Row, 1964), 232.

Saturday

1. Victor Hugo, *Les Miserables* (London: Penguin Books, 1987), 521.

2. W. A. Elwell, and P. W. Comfort, *Tyndale Bible Dictionary: Tyndale Reference Library* (Wheaton: Tyndale House Publishers, 2001), 1072.

3. Ibid.

4. See http://www.ancientdigger.com/2012/05/pompeii-erotic-art-and-roman-sexuality.html

5. Archibald Robertson, "1 Corinthians 6:18," *Word Pictures in the New Testament* (Nashville: Broadman Press), 1933.

6. J. C. Ryle, *Holiness* (Moscow: Charles Nolan Publishers, 2001), 64.

7. Everett F. Harrison, ed., *Bakers Dictionary of Theology* (Grand Rapids: Baker Book House, 1976), 112.

8. Dietrich Bonhoeffer, *Sanctorum Communio: A Theological Study of the Sociology of the Church* (DBW 1; ed. C. J. Green and J. von Soosten; translated by R. Krauss and N. Lukens) (Minneapolis: Fortress Press, 2009), 140.

9. P. P. Enns, *The Moody Handbook of Theology* (Chicago: Moody Press, 1989), 418.

10. Harrison, ed., *Bakers Dictionary of Theology*, 147.

11. J. I. Packer, *Growing in Christ* (Wheaton, IL: Crossway Books 1994).

Sunday

1. John Calvin, *Calvin's Commentaries on the Epistles of Paul to the Galatians and Ephesians*, vol. 21 (Grand Rapids: Baker Books, 2005), 178.

2. John Lukacs, *Blood, Toil, Tears and Sweat* (New York: Basic Books, 2008), 27.

3. Ibid., 26,

4. Roy Jenkins, *Churchill* (London: Macmillan, 2001), 592.

5. Lukacs, *Blood, Toil, Tears and Sweat*, 41.

6. See http://www.winstonchurchill.org/resources/speeches/1940-the-finest-hour/ blood-toil-tears-and-sweat

7. Rob Mackenzie, *David Livingstone: The Truth Behind the Legend* (Zimbabwe: Fig Tree Publications, 1993), 46.

8. Ibid.

9. Ibid.

10. Ibid.

11. James McPherson, *Abraham Lincoln* (New York: Oxford University Press, 2009), 30.

12. See http://www.abrahamlincolnonline.org/lincoln/speeches/house.htm

13. I pulled this from an excerpt off the Amazon website, http://www.amazon.com/ Team-Rivals-Political-Abraham-Lincoln/dp/0743270754

14. Doris Kearns Goodwin, *Team of Rivals* (New York: Simon &Schuster, 2005), 319.

15. Metaxas, *Seven Men*, 114.

16. Ibid., 124.

17. Ibid., 128.

18. Ibid., 62.

19. Ibid., 62.

20. Wilberforce and Wilberforce, *The Life of William Wilberforce*, 527.

21. Ibid., 528.

22. Hague, *William Wilberforce*, 503.

ABOUT THE AUTHOR

Brent Crowe is a thought-provoking visionary and speaker who has a passion to present the life-changing message of the gospel. Brent uses humor and real-life situations to relate to people at the heart of their struggles. The roles of husband, father, minister, evangelist, author, and leader have allowed Brent to influence people from all walks of life throughout his fifteen years in ministry.

Engaging issues such as leadership, culture, and change, Brent speaks to tens of thousands across the nation and abroad each year and is currently serving as vice president for Student Leadership University, a ministry that has trained over 140,000 students to think, dream, and lead at the feet of Jesus.

He is the author of *Reimagine: What the World Would Look Like If God Got His Way* and *Chasing Elephants: Wrestling with the Gray Areas of Life*. Additionally, Brent coauthored with David Nasser *The Call: God Is Calling . . . Will You Answer?* and is the Associate Editor of *IMPACT: The Student Leadership Bible*.

The desire of Brent's heart is to see people realize that they have been set apart to the gospel of God and thus, in turn, they must set their lives apart in an effort to capture every moment in worshipful service to Him.

Brent holds a doctorate in philosophy and two masters degrees (a masters of divinity in evangelism and a masters of arts in ethics) from Southeastern Baptist Theological Seminary. He and his wife, Christina, have three children, Gabriel, Charis, and Mercy.

www.slulead.com • www.brentcrowe.com

IF YOU ENJOYED THIS BOOK, WILL YOU CONSIDER SHARING THE MESSAGE WITH OTHERS?

Mention the book in a blog post or through Facebook, Twitter, Pinterest, or upload a picture through Instagram.

Recommend this book to those in your small group, book club, workplace, and classes.

Head over to facebook.com/brent.crowe.9, "LIKE" the page, and post a comment as to what you enjoyed the most.

Tweet "I recommend reading #SacredIntent by @BrentACrowe// @worthypub"

Pick up a copy for someone you know who would be challenged and encouraged by this message.

Write a book review online.

WORTHY®
PUBLISHING

Visit us at worthypublishing.com

twitter.com/worthypub

worthypub.tumblr.com

facebook.com/worthypublishing

pinterest.com/worthypub

instagram.com/worthypub

youtube.com/worthypublishing